The Mobile Commerce Revolution

Business Success in a Wireless World

TIM HAYDEN
TOM WEBSTER

800 East 96th Street,
Indianapolis, Indiana 46240 USA

The Mobile Commerce Revolution: Business Success in a Wireless World

ISBN-13: 978-0-78-975154-6
ISBN-10: 0-7897-5154-2

Library of Congress Control Number: 2014944846

Printed in the United States of America

First Printing: October 2014

Trademarks

Warning and Disclaimer

Special Sales

For information about buying this title in bulk quantities, or for special sales opportunities (which may include electronic versions; custom cover designs; and content particular to your business, training goals, marketing focus, or branding interests), please contact our corporate sales department at corpsales@pearsoned.com or (800) 382-3419.

For government sales inquiries, please contact governmentsales@pearsoned.com.

For questions about sales outside the U.S., please contact international@pearsoned.com.

Editor-in-Chief
Greg Wiegand

Senior Acquisitions Editor
Katherine Bull

Peer Reviewer
Tom Nawara

Development Editor
Karen Klein

Managing Editor
Kristy Hart

Project Editor
Elaine Wiley

Copy Editor
Geneil Breeze

Indexer
Lisa Stumpf

Proofreader
Paula Lowell

Publishing Coordinator
Kristen Watterson

Cover Designer
Mark Shirar

Compositor
Nonie Ratcliff

Que Biz-Tech Editorial Board
Michael Brito
Jason Falls
Rebecca Lieb
Simon Salt
Peter Shankman

CONTENTS

About the Author

Tim Hayden is Principal Strategist at TTH Strategy, a consultancy that provides guidance to organizations faced with business processes and communications challenges. He also serves as an investor and advisory board member to several ventures in cloud, mobile, and social technology. Prior to TTH Strategy, Tim led Edelman Digital's North American mobile program, and cofounded 44Doors, an SaaS mobile marketing platform. He was a founder and partner in other startups including NION Interactive and GamePlan, an experiential marketing agency that produced solutions for brands including AMD, Bacardi USA, Dell, Humana, and IBM using the integrated "Live+Mobile+Online" methodology that Tim coined in 2007. He is a graduate of Texas State University in San Marcos, Texas.

Tom Webster is Vice President of Strategy for Edison Research, a custom market research company best known as the sole providers of exit polling data during U.S. elections for all the major news networks. He has nearly 20 years of experience researching consumer usage of technology, new media, and social networking. Tom is the principal author of a number of widely cited studies, including "The Social Habit," "Twitter Users in America," and the coauthor of "The Infinite Dial," America's longest running research series on digital media consumption. He is a graduate of Tufts University in Medford, Massachusetts, and holds an MBA from the Bryan School of Business and Economics at the University of North Carolina.

Dedication

To our sons, Graeme and Sam, who may each prosper with a life full of adventurous experiences in the Age of Mobility.

Acknowledgments

From Tom:

I would like to thank Larry Rosin, Joe Lenski, and the amazing team at Edison Research, who always get it right.

To Tim Hayden, my brother from another mother, thank you for the opportunity, the prescience, the vision, and for trusting me. You made this book great, and I look forward to many years of CB lingo voice mail messages, good buddy.

Finally, to my constant beam, Tamsen Snyder Webster, who gave me support when I needed it, a kick when I deserved it, the gift of her miraculous brain, and all the inspiration I will ever need: Thank you, my great love.

From Tim:

In bars, ballrooms, and eateries around the world, Adam Beaugh, Matt Bruce, Stephanie Wonderlin Carls, Marcus Dyer, Spike Jones, Cierra Savatgy-King, Tony Long, Brad Mays, DJ Waldow, and others have each shaped my perspectives and passion for being human and living mobile. Thank you, all.

I've also been blessed by gracious opportunities to work alongside Sanjay Lall, Keith Dudley, and Andy Meadows, who are each responsible in part for everything I know and have proven in the worlds of marketing, mobility, and technology. Thank you, pardners.

Throughout writing this book, Tom Webster has been the support, wrangler, and brute force to make it real. The band will play on and on, and onward, compadre.

Not a word would be on these pages if my wife, Halea, did not let me gamble on new ventures, grant me her support, and extend her patience with me when there is no patience left to extend. She is My Love and my fuel for the long twisting road that is life, and the tank would be empty without her in my heart.

From Tim and Tom:

We thank Chris Brogan, who on one afternoon in 2008 in Dallas enabled the two of us to ignite our brotherly relationship, arguing over focus group efficacy in a world with real-time data, and four years later Jason Falls introduced us to Katherine Bull from Pearson with an idea for this book. You guys started this.

We want to acknowledge all the great advice we received from authors before us: Jay Baer, Tom Martin, C. C. Chapman, Ann Handley, Scott Stratten, Chuck Hemann, Ken Burbary, and Christopher S. Penn. Thank you, all.

Finally, we want to thank our wonderful editors at Pearson: Katherine Bull, Elaine Wiley, Karen Klein, and Mark Renfrow, and our technical editor, Tom Nawara. Thank you for making us look good.

We Want to Hear from You!

As the reader of this book, you are our most important critic and commentator. We value your opinion and want to know what we're doing right, what we could do better, what areas you'd like to see us publish in, and any other words of wisdom you're willing to pass our way.

As an associate publisher for Que Publishing, I welcome your comments. You can email or write me directly to let me know what you did or didn't like about this book—as well as what we can do to make our books better.

Please note that I cannot help you with technical problems related to the topic of this book. We do have a User Services group, however, where I will forward specific technical questions related to the book.

When you write, please be sure to include this book's title and author as well as your name, email address, and phone number. I will carefully review your comments and share them with the author and editors who worked on the book.

Email: feedback@quepublishing.com

Mail: Greg Wiegand
           Editor-in-Chief
           Que Publishing
           800 East 96th Street
           Indianapolis, IN 46240 USA

Reader Services

Visit our website and register this book at quepublishing.com/register for convenient access to any updates, downloads, or errata that might be available for this book.

Introduction

The title of this book uses a bold word: Revolution.

We often think about revolutions as political, religious, or socioeconomic debates that escalate into warfare. But a revolution can also apply to human behavior. All you need is for some kind of fundamental shift to happen, and for that shift to happen quickly. This book describes just such a shift—one that is happening rapidly and changing the face of worldwide cultures and economies, consumer attitudes, and business structure. We are now in the dawn of the mobile commerce revolution, complete with multisided battles, intense competition, and a hard-fought pursuit to define the future.

As you read in this book, the desktop era is dying. And along with its death and the growing maturation of the Age of Mobility, this new reality is set to alter everything.

Life changed dramatically with the advent of mobile phones, wireless Internet service, and a plethora of utilitarian apps available almost everywhere we go. Do you remember your first smartphone and the feeling of total liberation you felt? You were no longer tied to your office or home computer! You could check your email at lunch, or leave the office early, or let your spouse know you would be home late. In short, even then, smartphones changed your behavior.

As smartphones have become ubiquitous, however, they are used for far more than simply catching up with the office email. Today, we can negotiate prices with the babysitter via text message, pay the yard guy with PayPal, book a hotel that's nearby and vacant the moment we need it, and open a bar tab miles away to buy a friend a beer—from near anywhere at anytime.

Mobile technology has made a tremendous impact on our lives, and more disruption, both positive and challenging, is on the way. The revolution has just begun—and it's far more than simply a technological revolution.

Why We Wrote This Book

Las Vegas, Nevada, deserves much of the credit for Tim's fascination with mobile technology. In 2004, Tim attended the International Consumer Electronics Show (CES) for the first time. CES carries the reputation—true or not—of being North America's largest tradeshow and the world's "see-what-we've-been-dreaming-up" launch zone for consumer gadgets, appliances, and lifestyle electronics. Prior to attending, in August 2003, Tim sat in a small conference room in Overland Park, Kansas, where he was presenting a guerrilla marketing stunt idea to the Bluetooth Special Interest Group (SIG) that would steal the show at the 2004 CES. The effort was to drive awareness for Bluetooth-enabled products such as Logitech keyboards, the 2004 Acura, and new BMW models that would have the technology as a standard feature for hands-free cell phone use.

On that day in Kansas, though, Tim's views of marketing and consumer behavior were forever altered when one of the SIG board members told him that in parts of France and Scandinavia people already pay for groceries via Bluetooth. Some time later, another SIG board member told him that the Japanese were troubled with Bluetooth earpiece users because in Japanese culture you are considered crazy or possessed if you walk around talking to yourself. From that point on, Tim became much less focused on the technology and more focused on what people do—or don't do—with their newfound pocket computers.

In January 2007, Tim received a call from his then business partner, Keith Dudley, who was in San Diego to oversee the launch of Dell's sponsorship of Justin Timberlake's FutureSex/LoveSound tour. After seeing thousands of teenage girls at the event all capturing photos and video on their phones, Keith was struck with the potential opportunities provided through text messaging. He recognized that we could extend the experience before, during, and after the concert. At that moment, Tim and Keith shifted their entire view of event marketing, retail, and other live experiences. They saw it all as a *series of moments for a brand to be present.*

Tim's agency at the time, GamePlan, called it Live + Mobile + Online (see Figure 0.1).

Figure 0.1 *A simple illustration from 2007 to show the interdependence of offline experiences and digital media.*

It was precisely this complex interplay between online and offline behavior that first interested Tom. Tom has been tracking smartphone usage, consumer adoption of mobile technology, and the seismic shifts mobile technology caused in human behavior since 2006. As a professional market researcher, Tom began to realize that the increasing ubiquity of mobile technology was changing the ways in which people behave, and changing those behaviors faster than even the initial advent of the Internet did.

Much of Tom's work involves measuring advertising and marketing effectiveness on behalf of agencies and brands. One of the growing challenges faced by Tom's clients is the need to square all the online clickstream data that businesses are now "blessed" with having with consumer behavior in the *offline* world. In other words, did a banner ad that nobody clicked on (and is therefore seemingly ineffective) actually contain a message that drove someone to a retail location? Did an "untrackable" Twitter message influence someone's decision to test-drive a car? Calibrating online and offline data is one of the main challenges for any company that inhabits both spaces, and what Tom rapidly realized was that one of the keys to bridging the gaps between that data is mobile technology—after all, in many countries today, the majority of the population is *never* truly offline, thanks to the Internet in our pockets.

Where Tim and Tom violently agree is this: The ability to access information about nearly anything was just the beginning of the impact of the mobile Internet—the ability for a consumer to get the answer to a question nearly instantly, no matter where he is, has led to a behavioral shift in *other* things consumers expect to be able to do anywhere, anytime. And that has implications for business that go well beyond marketing.

It's Not Just Marketing

Mobile commerce is being defined with many different meanings by the most diverse system of stakeholders, not limited to incumbent technology vendors, bankers, retailers, advertising agencies, and aspiring 20-something technologists who've never run a business. We have friends and professional acquaintances who either fit or proudly wear many of these labels, and countless other social media networks, payment enablers, and telecom carriers claim they have it all figured out. There is no doubt that the battle will be long and fierce over the potential profits in mobile payments and transactions, and ultimately the customer will win.

Yet, the mobile commerce revolution is as much about society as it is about business. This may be lost on many who will either flourish or perish at the hands (and thumbs) of an always-on, always moving, untethered audience. From politics to travel to healthcare and retail, the world is undergoing a dramatic shift, thanks to widespread global adoption and usage of smartphones, tablet computers, and other mobile devices. This phenomenon is happening today and is not limited to the young or to the old, to the haves or to the have-nots, and this change does not discriminate by industry or tenure. The mobile commerce revolution affects us all, and there's no better time than now to begin to adapt to capitalize, survive, and succeed.

Mobile is a very deep and broad industry that grows and changes every day, if not every hour. Consider that year-over-year mobile data traffic grew 81% in 2013 (after growing 70% in 2012[1]), and more than 30% of smartphone users have owned their devices for less than 12 months.[2] You can see within those two numbers that mobile adoption is happening fast. Smartphone ownership has grown 500% in five years, and today 61% of Americans aged 12 years and older own a smartphone.[3]

---

1. Cisco Visual Networking Index: Global Mobile Data Traffic Forecast Update, 2012–2017 http://www.cisco.com/c/en/us/solutions/collateral/service-provider/visual-networking-index-vni/white_paper_c11-520862.html.

2. Edison Research, "The Smartphone Consumer 2012." http://www.edisonresearch.com/home/archives/2012/06/the-smartphone-consumer-2012.php#.U82FwWSwL6w.

3. "The Infinite Dial 2014," Edison Research and Triton Digital. http://www.edisonresearch.com/home/archives/2014/03/the-infinite-dial-2014.php#.U82GvmSwL6w

Consider that there are more mobile phones on the planet than there are people, and you cannot escape the conclusion that mobile is powering a fundamental shift in the way we shop, live, and communicate with each other.

Today, there is a land rush to build apps, software as a service (SaaS), payment, and media networks that create news and not-always warranted excitement for innovation and the future, unlike any industry in history. In fact, it's hard to even call mobile an "industry," which is why the title of this book invokes a better term: a revolution.

So, What Is This Book About, Really?

This book explains the vast changes to business associated with the adoption of mobile devices and their ubiquitous use. Case studies and expert viewpoints help you understand related challenges and opportunities and help you formulate solutions and tactics to leverage the age of mobility that is now upon us.

Yes, within these pages you find plenty of data to help you grasp the magnitude of smartphone (primarily) and tablet usage to find and buy things and make payments. However, in the words of the German poet Heinrich Heine, you cannot feed the hungry on statistics. Instead, we aim to provide the stories those numbers tell, and the decisions they may help you make.

If you own a business or are responsible in any way for either sales or marketing in someone else's business, this book helps you understand the dynamic shifts in consumer and purchase behavior resulting from wireless device use. Every business is different when it comes to audience or customer behavior and purchase habits, so our goal is to provide you with usable coordinates for weaving mobile technology and strategy into your marketing mix.

If you work for an agency or you are a consultant, this book helps you understand the urgency of advising clients with new strategies that address the aforementioned related challenges and opportunities. This may include direction on responsive web design, mobile applications, direct-response marketing, mobile payment solutions, and location-based tactics that leverage everything from Foursquare and Facebook to billboards and napkins.

We also include some case studies and stories for how brands such as Wells Fargo, Publicis Groupe, Torchy's Tacos, Diane von Furstenberg, and others, such as farmers in Kenya, are seeing success—and challenges—with their mobile investments.

And finally, our real goal with this book is not to help you with a "mobile strategy"—it's to get you to holistically consider your entire business differently and predict the future with a little more clarity. All of this and more is jam-packed into the next 19 chapters for you to learn how to capitalize at the intersection of mobile marketing and digital commerce.

1

The Current State of Mobile

Here's a prediction: Right now, as you are reading this, you are within arm's reach of a smartphone. How did we do? To be honest, it wasn't a difficult prediction to make. Today, the majority of Americans own a smartphone, and 83% of them say they are always or nearly always within reach of their mobile device. You can walk into a convenience store, buy a prepaid, no-contract smartphone for under $100, and have the Internet in your pocket.

For years, technologists have been talking about "convergence" devices—technology that replaces two or more gadgets and gizmos. The smartphone has truly become the ultimate convergence device. Think about the devices it has replaced: media players, navigation devices, guidebooks, your wallet, and even your desktop computer. The smartphone has quickly become all these things.

Smartphones have also effectively ended the bar bet. Remember Norm and Cliff from the television series *Cheers*? Cliff's character, a mailman played by John Ratzenberger, was often the instigator and arbiter of trivia questions at the show's eponymous bar. Today, however, we are *all* Cliff. The answer to nearly any trivia question is just a mobile search away. In fact, having the answers in our pocket to "who sang that song?" and "who was that actor?" has conditioned us to expect the answers to nearly everything, whenever and wherever we need them. And that has changed our behavior, as we discuss later in the book.

Americans and Smartphones

Tom's company, Edison Research, has been tracking mobile phone ownership, usage, and other mobile behaviors for nearly a decade in its annual Infinite Dial study, a long-running research series that has been providing representative data about technology and media usage in America since 1998. In the most recent Infinite Dial study from 2014, an estimated 160 million Americans, or 61% of Americans aged 12 and older, now own a smartphone (defined as an Android, iOS, Blackberry, or Windows-based phone). What this number masks, however, are some significant demographic and psychographic differentials in smartphone ownership. In fact, the numbers for smartphone ownership for people aged 12 to 34 are truly staggering—more than three-quarters in that demographic (and 74% of teens!) own a smartphone.

What's truly interesting about smartphones (as compared to feature phones, which are non-smart phones without Internet access) is that a new generation of users has become as comfortable communicating with their thumbs as with their voices. When we asked mobile phone users how often they send or receive text messages on their phones, 75% of smartphone owners said several times per day, compared to just 29% of feature phone owners. Is this because smartphone owners are more communicative? Possibly, but unlikely. It's far more likely the power of a smartphone and the increased usage of apps on the mobile Internet makes users increasingly comfortable keeping the phone in front of them, rather than glued to their ear.

Indeed, we now have many means of communication available that simply didn't exist five years ago. Consider apps like Instagram and Snapchat. Three in 10 smartphone owners have Instagram accounts, making the company's $1 billion sale to Facebook look like a bargain in retrospect, especially when you consider that Facebook paid $19 billion for the messaging app WhatsApp. Snapchat, which has only been around for three years as of this writing, is now used by 19% of smartphone users. In fact, as shown in Figure 1.1, nearly half of 12- to 24-year-olds use Snapchat (so the odds are good that your teenager does, too). Both services now

tap into tens of millions of users who are using their phones to share images, messages, and above all, experiences in altogether new ways.

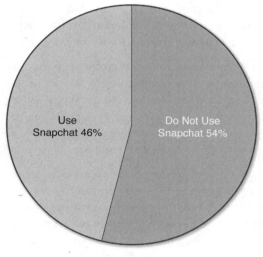

Nearly Half of 12-24s Use Snapchat
% Age 12-24 Who Ever Use Snapchat

Use Snapchat 46%

Do Not Use Snapchat 54%

©Edison Research and Triton Digital

Figure 1.1   *Snapchat usage amongst Americans 12-24*

Nowhere is this more apparent than in the use of social media. An incredible 40%
of social media users with smartphones check those sites and services *several times
per day*. This translates to some fairly remarkable behaviors. For example, the average smartphone owner who has a profile on Facebook checks his account six times
per day, and 60% of them say they access Facebook *most* via mobile phone.

Previously, we noted that 83% of smartphone owners have their phones nearly
always within arm's reach. This has resulted in many tens of millions relying on
the phone as the first thing they look at in the morning (ostensibly after their
spouse, as applicable)—indeed, for many smartphone owners, it is their device that
actually wakes them up, replacing the clock radio. In fact, when asked what media
they typically consume *most* at home in the morning, 24% of smartphone users
indicated that it is their mobile device, second only to their television at 27%.

Of course, these stats can be slightly deceptive—after all, the smartphone has
become the television, the radio, and the newspaper for so many. For the first time
since Edison Research started tracking this stat in 2005, iPod ownership has actually declined, from 31% in 2013 to 29% in 2014. Today's smartphone owners have

started to essentially replace their dedicated music players with their phones, and as a result, their media consumption habits have also changed.

For example, have you ever listened to a podcast? Before smartphones became so ubiquitous, mobile consumption of a podcast consisted of downloading a media file to your desktop or laptop, and then transferring it over to a portable media player to listen to it on the go. Today, all the friction has gone out of this process. In 2014, for the first time, most podcast users report that they listen primarily to podcasts on their mobile devices, and not on a computer.

Smartphones have opened up media consumption opportunities for audio, video, and text that heretofore never existed (or were at least difficult propositions). YouTube videos, Netflix movies, Pandora radio stations—all are available at the touch of an app, on the bus, at the gym, and even at the bar, next to Cliff. In fact, 50% of all smartphone owners have downloaded the Pandora app, an estimated 80 million Americans aged 12+—a staggering number for an individual brand.

Nowhere are those increased consumption opportunities more apparent than in the car. The connected dashboard may or may not be a feature in your next car, but the fact is—it's already here for smartphone owners. In fact, 26% of mobile phone owners have listened to Internet radio in the car by connecting their phones to their vehicles (either through Bluetooth, or simply through a cable in an auxiliary jack). This number has grown significantly over the past few years, as you can see in Figure 1.2.

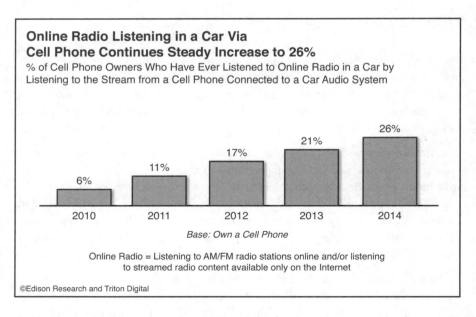

Figure 1.2 *In-car usage of Internet Radio*

This has opened up a world of opportunity for media producers to have their content consumed in new places, in new settings, and by multiple people (by freeing their content from the confines of the earbud). As a result, overall media consumption continues to rise; we are consuming media nearly every waking moment.

Mobile Around the World

The mobile revolution is a truly global revolution; indeed, Cisco's 2014 Global Mobile Data Traffic Forecast shows that global mobile data usage increased by 81% year-over-year from 2012 to 2013.[1] Indeed, while North America continues to see significant growth, Cisco reports even higher growth percentages in Asia, and continuing growth throughout the developing world, as Figure 1.3 illustrates.

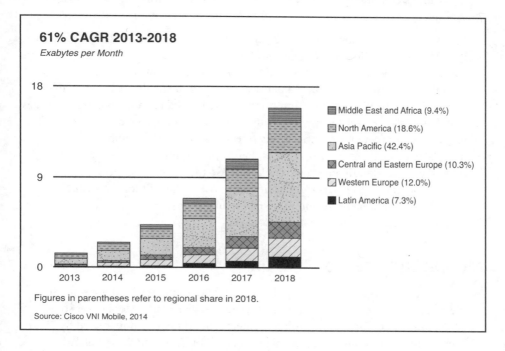

Figure 1.3   *The compound annual growth rate (CAGR) in mobile data usage listed in exabytes (one exabyte=one billion gigabytes). Note the significant CAGR in the Asia Pacific region.*

The really intriguing statistic in this report, however, lies in the distribution of mobile data. In 2013, the top 1% of mobile data users globally generated 10% of

---

1. Cisco Visual Networking Index: Global Mobile Data Traffic Forecast Update, 2013–2018.

mobile data traffic. This is actually down 50% since 2010. What does this mean? Simply put, the evening out of mobile data usage worldwide indicates that more and more people are relying on their smartphones for everyday Internet-related tasks, reducing the relative contribution of the most active users.

The International Telecommunication Union (ITU) recently published some statistics on global mobile technology penetration. According to its most recent report,[2] there are now 6.8 billion mobile-cellular subscriptions—almost one for every human on the planet. In fact, in developed nations, there is more than one mobile phone per resident (128%), with developing nations not far behind (89%).

Mobile broadband subscriptions have also grown tremendously, at a rate of 40% per year from 2007 to 2013. While overall penetration of mobile broadband is lower in developing nations, there we see the highest growth rate, with Africa (for example) realizing 82% annual growth in mobile broadband from 2010 to 2013.

Much has been said about the "platform wars" between Google's Android, Apple's iOS, Microsoft's Windows Mobile, and BlackBerry OS, and the statistics here vary considerably. While "usage" shows iOS as the leading mobile operating system, sales figures show Android-based phones outselling the field by a considerable margin in 2013.[3] What is more important, however, than simply looking at phones as iOS devices, or Android devices, is this: They are all Internet devices. According to the Pew Internet and American Life research series, 34% of mobile Internet users admit that their mobile phone is their primary Internet access device,[4] a trend that is accelerating even faster globally. So the intense competition between mobile operating systems is truly having one positive benefit for the world: As these devices become more and more powerful and easy to use, they are truly putting the Internet into the world's pockets.

Mobile Commerce

Mobile penetration has grown rapidly, but mobile commerce is where some truly eye-popping figures can be found. In Internet Retailer's 2014 Mobile 500 study, 2013 mobile sales for the 500 largest retailers around the world increased by 71% over the same period in 2012, reaching $30.5 billion (up from $17.8 billion). Consider this stat for a moment. A growth rate of 71% for mobile retail commerce is significantly higher than the growth rate for mobile phone penetration. We can draw two conclusions here: First, more companies are making their wares available

---

2. The World in 2013: ITC Facts and Figures, The International Telecommunications Union.

3. Net Applications, *Mobile OS Market Share as of February 2014* and Gartner, *Mobile OS Market Share as of 2nd quarter 2013*.

4. The Pew Internet and American Life Study, 2013.

to sell via mobile channels. And second, consumers are becoming more comfortable making mobile purchases. Indeed, for many retailers, mobile is not only their biggest growth engine, it's becoming their biggest segment of sales, period.

In fact, we can already see mobile commerce behaviors becoming preeminent if we look at shopping traffic patterns. A 2013 study from Shop.org, The Partnering Group, and comScore revealed that 55% of the time spent on retailers' websites was from mobile devices, compared to 45% from traditional computers.[5] Clearly, while actual mobile sales are a significant driver for commerce, mobile shopping is even more important.

Finally, it is worth noting this stat, from Nielsen, which shows that 72% of smartphone shoppers who make a purchase on their device do so *at home*, not "out and about."[6] This is an important point when putting what we think of as mobile commerce into perspective. What the smartphone and other mobile Internet devices enable is more than just "out of home" commerce. What mobile technology makes possible is commerce wherever, and whenever, the buyer deems appropriate.

Beyond the Numbers

These statistics are important, but what do they mean? We've seen substantial growth rates for any number of technologies, channels, and platforms over the past few decades, but mobile is outpacing them all. Any kind of statistical analysis has to also recognize the rapid, dramatic rise in mobile-related behaviors. When we learn that 26% of mobile phone users have hooked up their phones to their cars to listen to media, this shows more than simply a typical adoption curve for new technology. It shows a clear, pent-up demand to engage in activities previously not possible, but certainly imagined. After all, it isn't necessarily a straightforward activity to connect your phone to a vehicle, and yet tens of millions of Americans have done just that to have more choice and control over the content they want to consume.

The rise in smartphone ownership, and the even more dramatic rise in mobile-related behaviors, is not just about technology. It's about enabling behaviors that are natural to humans, and there's no better way to think about them than to imagine a day in the life of a modern smartphone user.

First of all, how do you wake up in the morning? In 2013, Edison's Infinite Dial study asked that question of a representative sample of Americans aged 12 and older. The number one answer, at 30% of the population, was by setting an alarm

---

5. 2013 Social & Mobile Commerce Report, 2013, Shop.org, The Partnering Group, and comScore.
6. "A Mobile Shopper's Journey: From the Couch to the Store (and Back Again)," 2013, Nielsen.

on a mobile phone.[7] Remember the movie *Groundhog Day*, in which Bill Murray's character kept waking up on the same calendar day to a radio morning show? Today, a plurality of Americans wake up to a *noise*—the noise of their smartphone alarm.

After shaking off the cobwebs of sleep, today's smartphone owner takes the phone off the nightstand and checks Facebook, the emails that came in the night before, the weather, and the news headlines. Statistically, smartphone owners check Facebook several more times throughout the day, because they *can*. But for now, a simple scan will do.

After breakfast, our mobile-savvy consumer gets dressed, packs his bag for the day, and turns once again to the mobile phone. For those who commute by car, a destination is loaded into a navigation app that features a real-time traffic subscription, informing of the fastest route to work. For those who take public transportation, apps are available that transmit the exact times that the bus or the subway will arrive, and the optimal path for the commuter to use to get in on time and with no wasted effort.

During the commute, either via car or public transportation, the smartphone user consumes media previously unavailable. Drivers listen to Pandora or a Spotify playlist. Bus riders listen to yesterday's NPR podcasts, or watch a news program on YouTube or Hulu. Some may even share a funny moment from those shows over Twitter, or snap a photo of their commute to post to Instagram, a behavior that was not possible just three years ago.

Before entering the office, our protagonist walks by a coffee shop. Just by passing through the doorway, a Near Field Communications (NFC) or Bluetooth Low-Energy (BLE) chip notifies the coffee shop that a Cafe Americano is on order, and a connected mobile wallet takes care of the bill. Not a word is spoken as the exact order is placed, retrieved, and consumed.

That morning, our subject may work on a variety of tasks, online and off, but he takes a number of "digital vacations" at various times throughout the day. Many of these breaks take the form of checking Facebook or other social media platforms. At one point, our hero sees a friend post about a new music recording, or a book, or a movie. In that instant, a decision is made, and the book or the album, is seamlessly purchased and downloaded to the phone.

Halfway through the day, our hero finishes downloading the new book or music and decides to go out to lunch. A location-based application finds a nearby restaurant, and another app secures a reservation without so much as a phone call.

7. The Infinite Dial 2013, Edison Research and Arbitron.

During lunch, the smartphone is retrieved once again, to submit a review of the restaurant on Yelp, or simply to check in on Swarm to let friends know the best place for a hot dog downtown.

After lunch, on the walk back to the office, our hero hears about a new TV show and searches his phone for the details. After reading several positive reviews, he orders a few episodes, or even a whole season, to watch on the way home. A text is sent to a spouse: "Pizza and a movie?" "Good idea!" By the time the commute home rolls around, the movie is ready to go and dinner is ordered for pickup via a mobile app.

During the movie, a product placement shows up for a new sports car. Once again, the smartphone is employed, and several reviews of the car are found while sitting on the couch. A decision is made: A test-drive seems like a good idea. An appointment is made via email with a local dealer during the movie, and another app is consulted to line up possible financing.

Finally, it's time for bed. An alarm is set on the phone, tomorrow's weather consulted, and a conversation with a spouse points the way to a book that a son or daughter spoke about. The phone is brought out once again, and an order placed with an online retailer; the book will arrive in two days. The lights go out, and our hero goes to bed, to sleep the sleep of champions.

None of what you have just read was possible even five years ago. And yet, nothing here is science fiction or implausible—only new ways to do the things we've always done, like order pizza. That is the point of this chapter: The advances in mobile technology are not about enabling things that were previously unimaginable. These things were all imaginable. What mobile technology enables is the ability to do things where and when we want to do them, plain and simple, and that as much as anything has led to the dramatic rise in smartphone ownership and usage over the past three years. Smartphones make doing the things we already do even easier.

The current state of mobile does not enable some strange or foreign activity, but the ability to engage in the familiar, no matter where we are. In fact, the mobile commerce revolution is not about technology, but rather about what we can *do* with that technology, and how it enables and empowers us to engage in natural behaviors that we didn't even know we could engage in. If you travel to a new city and wonder where you should go for dinner, you've never had more information at your fingertips than you do right now, and mobile technology is a great equalizer in that sense. With near-perfect information available at our fingertips in terms of local business reviews, for instance, the best "mobile" strategy for a restaurant is to be a great restaurant, period. Thanks to mobile review and reservation apps, there's simply no other way to survive in a world with near-perfect, instant, real-time communication.

The Bottom Line

The advances in mobile technology over the past five years are unlike any other advances seen before. Some technological advances open our eyes to things we never dreamed we could do, or even had the language to describe. That's not what mobile technology is about. Instead, the statistics in this chapter underline what is truly powerful about mobile technology: It's not about enabling things we couldn't have imagined. Instead, today's mobile technology enables exactly what the average consumer *could* have imagined, albeit in settings and situations that could not have been predicted.

Mobile technology, and mobile broadband in particular, enables us to consume media, purchase products, and, yes, settle bar bets in situations that were not possible a few years ago. In short, mobile enhances our everyday lives in ways that many of us now take for granted, which is truly remarkable for a technology that is only a few years old. We grew up watching Cliff on *Cheers* telling us about the Egyptians, how World War I started, or the history of capitalism. Today, in the great meritocracy of the mobile world, we *all* have access to that information. The bar bet is over. And the great mobile commerce revolution is just beginning.

2

Mobile Is a Behavior, Not a Technology

All you have to do is walk down a busy street, through an airport, or into a retail store, and you can see that the majority of the people around you carry a mobile phone. Prior to the release of the first iPhone on June 29, 2007, most of these people would probably be holding their mobile device to their ear, talking or listening. Maybe you would have seen some text messaging (more on SMS and MMS messaging can be found in Chapter 15, "Email and Text Messaging"). You might have even seen a few BlackBerry owners checking their corporate mail.

That's what we knew mobile phones to be: a simple, wireless, one-to-one connection that enabled us to remotely conduct conversations with friends, family, and companies. Today, though, the majority of people around us may be looking down at their smartphones as much as they are listening to music through earphones or making calls with them. And the things those people do with those phones are, in many case, things we could not have imagined just five years ago.

The smartphone's gift to humanity is that of an untethered life, where mobile users are liberated from prolonged hours of desktop computing with anytime, anywhere access to information, entertainment, productivity, communications, and commerce. Depending on your personal routine and business perspective, you may believe that the majority of activity on smartphones is for entertainment, sending and receiving email or text messages, or perhaps wasting away hours of the day viewing the newsfeed of a popular social media network. And, while all of the above may label how many of us spend a chunk of our time using these magical handheld supercomputers that we call "phones," we are also reshaping our personal, professional, and consumer behaviors.

A number of perspectives help marketers and businesses understand what is happening with individual users when looking at the rapid adoption of smartphones. There is certainly a growing dependency on our mobile phones, as we can see from the potentially surprising responses to a few simple poll questions:

- We know that most people would rather lose their wallet than lose their mobile phone, if faced with such an option. Survey after survey on the topic reveals that not only would the loss of the phone "hurt" more than the loss of the wallet, the phone wins by a large margin. This is logical, since you can make calls to cancel credit cards and report the wallet stolen from the phone, but you can't use your wallet to call and report the theft of your phone!

- A June 2012 study from Lookout/Harris Interactive revealed that nearly six in ten smartphone-owning respondents don't go *an hour* without checking their phones, and 73% felt "panicked" when they misplaced their devices.

- We know that we hardly ever leave home without our mobile phones. We actually hardly leave the room without our mobile phones, as research from an Edison Research study in early 2013 shows that 83% of American (12+ years of age) mobile phone owners are "Sometimes" to "Always" within arm's reach of that device, as shown in Figure 2.1.

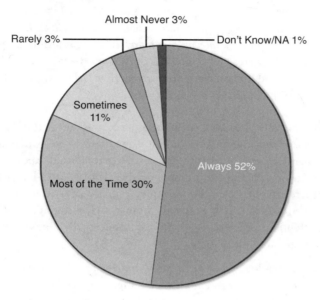

How often is your cell phone with you or nearby, that is, when it is within arm's reach?

Almost Never 3%

Rarely 3%

Don't Know/NA 1%

Sometimes 11%

Always 52%

Most of the Time 30%

Figure 2.1 *Responses from mobile phone owners aged 12 years and older in the United States when asked how often they have their mobile phone within arm's reach.*

There are, of course, some implications to our mobile addiction. Maura Nevel Thomas is the founder and chief trainer of RegainYourTime.com and the creator of the Empowered Productivity System, a process for managing the details of life and work. She was first introduced to us as someone who could "help you manage your time and make sense of the mess on your desk." Few people study and know how technology has changed human behavior over the past 20 years as much as Maura. Here's what she had to say about how smartphones are rewiring our brains:

> The opportunities for mobile and social technology to enhance our lives are exciting, and they should continue to add convenience and utility, and revolutionize the consumer buying experience. These possibilities also come with a potential danger, however: the ability of ever-present technology to feed our "addiction to distraction," and rob us of the richness of the present moment. Having the world at our fingertips (or on our wrists, or eyes) in terms of our mobile devices

makes it increasingly tempting to indulge most any whim of our imagination, sometimes continually: *Any good news in my email? What's the weather going to be? What's my calendar look like for tomorrow? Has anyone commented on my post on Facebook/Twitter/LinkedIn? What are my friends up to? What's on sale today?* The list is limitless, and is contributing to increasing symptoms of ADD in the general public. This is evidenced by noted attention researcher Dr. Edward Hallowell's phrase, *culturally induced ADD.*[1]

Indeed, according to the 2013 Mobile Consumer Habits study from Jumio/Harris Interactive, 55% of smartphone users admit using their devices while driving, 33% on a dinner date, and nearly one in ten smartphone users admitted to using their phones during sex (and that number doubles with 18- to 34-year-olds).[2] We submit that there aren't many other technologies that can lay claim to those kinds of statistics. The rewiring of our brains by mobile devices doesn't simply mean we have less attention for websites; we are continuously dividing our attention between those sites and our real life.

This always-on dependency that some call a *smartphone obsession* presents a marked shift in our routines and ability to be attentive. While this may certainly mean that there are more direct channels and opportunities for marketers to provide utility to customers, influence brand preference, and drive sales, it is important to note that shifts in audience attention, routines, and habits also shape the success (or failure) of certain mobile marketing and commerce efforts.

Brands and marketers must know that before getting into technology, creative or strategic exercises, a thorough understanding of each market segment's behavior, mobile proficiency, and adoption rates is critical for budgeting and plotting success. Figure 2.2 is an illustration of the three classifications of mobile use and addiction that can occur with various combinations of socioeconomic status, age, profession, and length of device ownership.

Today, many consumers are acquiring their first smartphone, and many existing smartphone owners are acquiring their second or third device to replace what they are carrying today. Another interesting look into mobile behavior is in understanding how a smartphone user gains comfort and proficiency with a new device, whether their first smartphone or a replacement, as shown in Figure 2.3.

---

1. Unless otherwise noted, quoted material and information from businesspersons comes from interviews conducted by the authors.

2. http://pages.jumio.com/rs/jumio/images/Jumio%20-%20Mobile%20Consumer%20Habits%20Study-2.pdf

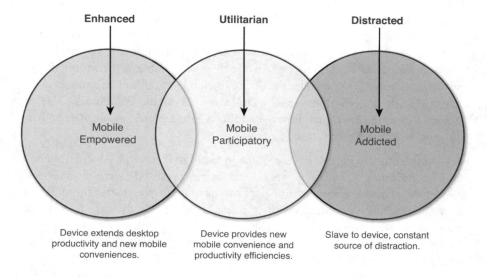

Figure 2.2   *The three stages of smartphone use and addiction.*

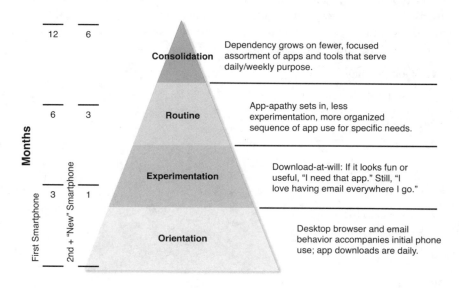

Figure 2.3   *Mobile users gain comfort and confidence in using a new smartphone.*

Figure 2.3 shows that not only do behavioral shifts happen quickly for smartphone owners, they happen at least twice as quickly for people buying their second or third device. And while the marketplace is flooded with thousands of mobile apps and services, users quickly coalesce on a fairly small number as their proficiency with the technology approaches the Consolidation level. Indeed, this mirrors Internet usage patterns uncovered by Dr. Jeffrey Cole at the USC Annenberg School Center for the Digital Future that shows Internet users spend 90% of their time on just 15 different websites.[3]

So, consider that in light of the top of the pyramid in Figure 2.3. As smartphone users rapidly pare down the apps and tools they use to suit their mobile lives, earning a spot on a smartphone's home page means more than just what technologies consumers can and do interact with; it means knowing what they are doing while mobile, and why they are doing it. These behaviors vary by demographic and psychographic cohort, geographic region, societal norms, and other cultural phenomena. Knowing that information is a competitive advantage—and a mobile strategy has to incorporate far more than simply adjusting how your website displays on a smartphone.

Finally, to come full circle from how mobile phones *used* to be used to how they are used today, consider this list of the top 10 most used apps in the world, ordered by percentage of global smartphone users who used those apps in the last month, from GlobalWebIndex's 3Q 2013 study:[4]

1. Google Maps
2. Facebook
3. YouTube
4. Google+
5. Twitter
6. Skype
7. Facebook Messenger
8. WhatsApp
9. Amazon
10. Ebay

What is remarkable about this list is just how many of these apps are used to ostensibly engage in the behaviors we opened this chapter with—communicating with

---

3. The Digital Future Project 2013, USC Annenberg School Center for the Digital Future.

4. https://www.globalwebindex.net/products/report/stream-report-device-q3-2013

people. But non-smartphones were used to engage in synchronous, one-to-one conversations. You stopped what you were doing and engaged in a conversation at that time and place—something you might have been reluctant to do while out with friends, or dinner, or at a sporting event.

The majority of the apps in this list, however, allow a behavior never before possible—the ability to communicate asynchronously with groups of family, friends, and colleagues, and to share more than just voice and text. Today, our ability to quickly post where we are, what we are doing, and even images of our surroundings—all without really interrupting those activities—enables us to share experiences with other humans in ways never before possible. The phone has moved in just a few short years from being an annoyance during those occasions, to a mandatory part of those occasions. When Ellen DeGeneres took a "selfie" photograph of her standing next to a number of Hollywood stars at the 2014 Oscars, she captured a moment and shared that moment with millions of people instantly. Millions of humans do the exact same thing, all around the world, every day.

The smartphone is the catalyst behind our newfound desire to connect and share experiences on social networking sites and services, and the demographic differences in some of these behaviors are striking. Consider the graph in Figure 2.4, which shows the relative usage of a variety of social sites and services with Americans ages 12 to 24.

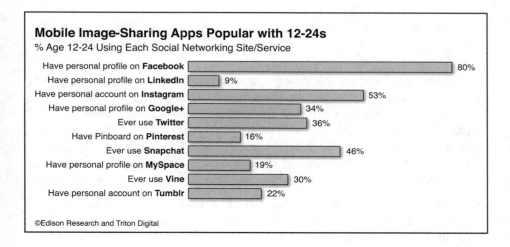

Mobile Image-Sharing Apps Popular with 12-24s
% Age 12-24 Using Each Social Networking Site/Service

- Have personal profile on **Facebook** — 80%
- Have personal profile on **LinkedIn** — 9%
- Have personal account on **Instagram** — 53%
- Have personal profile on **Google+** — 34%
- Ever use **Twitter** — 36%
- Have Pinboard on **Pinterest** — 16%
- Ever use **Snapchat** — 46%
- Have personal profile on **MySpace** — 19%
- Ever use **Vine** — 30%
- Have personal account on **Tumblr** — 22%

©Edison Research and Triton Digital

Figure 2.4   *Percentage of Americans ages 12 to 24 who use various social sites and services, taken from The Infinite Dial 2014 by Edison Research and Triton Digital.*

Yes, Facebook is number one, but the next two are Instagram at 53% of 12- to 24-year-olds and Snapchat at 46% of 12- to 24-year olds. That's roughly half of teens and young adults sharing images and messages with groups of friends in ways that did not even exist five years ago. And there is no reason to think that those behaviors will not stay with them as they age into other demographics. Consider the graph in Figure 2.5 from the same study.

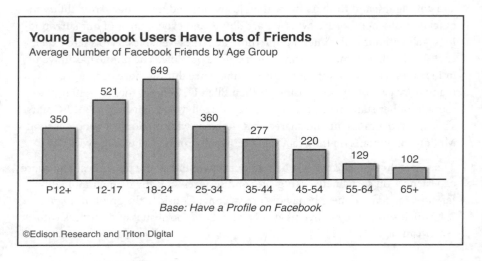

Figure 2.5   *Younger Americans have significantly more social connections than other age groups.*

This graph clearly shows that younger Americans have many more connections. Whether you consider those connections strong bonds or weak ties, one thing is clear: As those users age in to other demographics, many of those connections and the desire to share information with them will go right along with them. Mobile devices facilitate and encourage these connections and the sharing of experiences. Indeed, while 28% of Americans 12+ years old check their social networking sites and services several times daily, that number rises to 39% with smartphone users.[5]

So, why would a smartphone user want to take a mobile picture of herself and share it with the world? At least part of the answer: because she can. Understanding why we do the things we do with our smartphones, and what we might want to do with them in the future, is the central challenge—and opportunity—of the mobile commerce revolution.

---

5. The Infinite Dial 2014 from Edison Research and Triton Digital.

What Does Behavior Have to Do with Marketing and Business?

Preparing for the wider adoption and usage of smartphones by customers and prospective customers requires a business to adjust its culture and approach to service as much as its technology. Expectations and preferences will be formed around what mobile technology empowers users to do for *themselves*, and the next five years will bring substantial shifts in communication and shopping behavior. In Chapters 10 through 18, a more tactical look is presented for what can be done to make a business mobile-ready and mobile-optimized for these shifts.

While things are sure to change over time with greater mobility and new-fangled technology in the hands of consumers, a pragmatic approach to mobile marketing may be ideal. Some businesses and industries may only need to stick to fundamental marketing practices, motivating mobile users with promotions, and providing timely information in a way that is tailored to the devices they are using. Immediate success will not always involve reinventing the wheel or mastering new technology; it comes from making sure that mobile users are served with content that adapts to their devices and locations and that gives them the feeling of a personalized shopping experience.

To this, we would add one more simple adaption: Content (and applications) must be served that not only adapts to devices and location, but also to context—that is, what are mobile users likely to be doing when they access your company's mobile presence, what are they likely to want, and how can you provide that value efficiently (and delightfully). In short, a successful mobile strategy may take varying devices and technologies into account, but the starting point must always be what people expect to be able to do with that technology.

The ubiquitous and pervasive reality of smartphone use will require many brands to move in a direction where business rules are set for marketing coordinated by location, time of day, customer data, and an overall need to be relevant and personalized at every touch point possible. This may sound like a challenge, and in fact it is—if you start with the technology and not the human. If you start with the behavior—what humans want or expect to do while they are mobile—it won't be just a mobile strategy that you develop. You might just rethink your whole business.

3

The Collapsing Sales Funnel

Just as consumers have evolved in response to mobility, the ways in which humans do business is also changing. In a widely cited statistic from Google's Zero Moment of Truth, the number of pieces of information that the average consumer consults before making a purchase doubled in just one year-from just over five in 2010, to more than 10 in 2011.[1] The reason is pretty simple, and it's the same reason behind the sharing of selfies discussed in the previous chapter: Because we can.

There has been a lot of discussion around the concept of showrooming, the phenomenon by which a consumer visits an offline retailer, uses a mobile device to compare prices online, and then buys the item elsewhere (and presumably at an online retailer). A study conducted in January 2013 by Placed revealed that yes, this behavior certainly takes place, and big-box brands like BestBuy, Sears, and Barnes & Noble are among the brands that showrooming impacts the most.[2] But pricing data is not the only thing being researched on mobile phones.

1. Jim Lecinski, *Winning the Zero Moment of Truth*, http://www.thinkwithgoogle.com/collections/zero-moment-truth.html
2. "White Paper: Aisle to Amazon," Placed.com. http://www.placed.com/resources/white-papers/aisle-to-amazon

There is other, compelling research from the Interactive Advertising Bureau (IAB) that showrooming also fuels impulse purchases in-store. A 2013 study conducted for the IAB by Ipsos revealed that 32% of persons using mobile devices while shopping had made an impulse buy in store, compared to 7% of persons who do not consult mobile devices while shopping, and that the biggest in-store spenders did research on their mobile devices.[3] Clearly, pricing data is not the only information that mobile-empowered shoppers are seeking, and the fact that there are both product research behaviors *and* mobile-assisted impulse buys taking place reveals the complexity (and, again, the changes in consumer behavior) involved with mobile commerce.

Mobile technology is helping shoppers become better educated, and as a result, subverting the traditional notion of "the sales funnel." Everyone in business at one time or another attempts to draw a pathway or journey for how sales are generated, and how consumers commit to purchases. We try to think of it in a linear manner that can be translated as a timeline, in a spreadsheet, or illustrated as a sales funnel. Marketers and sales executives put together steps or episodes for the *when* and *where* they could best engage or reach a target audience. Mobile usage, however, is disrupting many of these models, if not all, constantly redrawing the lines that have made planning marketing and media a somewhat more predictable exercise. That exercise in planning what to execute, and when to execute it, was formerly mapped to what we believed as certainty in the decision processes and purchase behavior of customers. Today, however, businesses have to plan for a customer base that can consult reviews, sales information, and recommendations from their friends, anywhere and anytime.

In 2006–2007 we began to see how social media and mobile phone use disrupted so much of this and how those two forces would continue to bend the pathways of sales and the purchase journey. Even with the initial widespread use of social media, we still had confidence that most customers and prospects were sitting at a desk, staring at email, a browser, or a document for most of their "awake" or "office" hours. Back then, it was only through extreme raw manual coding of rudimentary data and observations that we were able to track and measure the time and distance it took to reach marketing targets and convert them into a sales system. Figure 3.1 illustrates an example of how this was illustrated for clients who wanted to leverage events and retail promotions as part of a larger campaign.

The diagram in Figure 3.1 makes the assumption that a marketing effort starts with a place or moment controlled or defined by media, data, or a customer relationship management (CRM) system. With mobile, the "start" can still be planned around known marketing or media touch points, yet also be ignited by something more

---

3. "Showrooming: Empowering Consumer Electronics Shoppers," IAB/IPSOS. http://www.iab.net/ showrooming

passive, such as a memory or impulse conversation with a friend, or something overheard in a bar or in an elevator.

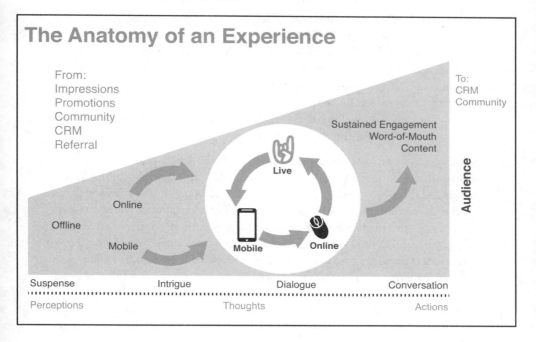

Figure 3.1 *"The Anatomy of an Experience," an image that Tim shared with many clients and prospects to illustrate how experiential marketing (events, live promotions, sponsorship activations, and digital media) could be extended before and after a live experience using digital media. (Credit: GamePlan, Keith Dudley)*

Consider, then, that showrooming is not the only prepurchase mobile interaction that a consumer might have with a brand. Imagine that you are in that bar, or elevator, and you hear a friend or colleague recommend a product. You then take out your smartphone, conduct a mobile search for the product's website, and maybe read one or two online reviews of that product. Based on that information, you then navigate to Amazon.com or another mobile retailer, and purchase the product.

What is notable about this interaction is that the brand's communications played a limited role in the consumer journey. Awareness was not driven by a brand communication, nor did some form of advertising influence the purchase decision. Instead, an offline communication with a friend led directly to a mobile purchase, and whatever plans the brand might have had for the "order" of consumer messages went completely out the window. The consumer went from awareness to consideration to purchase, but in a radically different way than ever before. And it is this kind of casual elevator mention of a product or brand that mobile has turned into the new impulse buy.

If marketers begin to think this way, newspaper circulars and magazines are still powerful. When people read the newspaper—and a lot of people still do read the paper, magazines, and direct mail—a mobile phone is always within a few feet, as we've seen from the research presented in Chapter 2, "Mobile Is a Behavior, Not a Technology." This device increasingly is a smartphone capable of making a call, searching the Web, sending email, and more—in fact, as mobile apps continue to evolve, there is nearly no limit to the quality and quantity of interactions a brand can have with a mobile-empowered consumer.

Brands can now activate otherwise passive print media with calls-to-action such as downloading a coupon, subscribing to an email list, or following a brand in social media, and these behaviors can be tracked. And, although it is not yet widely seen in practice, consumers carrying the latest model of smartphones will soon be recognized and rewarded with deals as they walk down the street, down an aisle at the local grocer, and as they visit a specific department in a retail store. If they "opt in" to email, text messaging, or app notifications, these deals and offers will be pushed to the smartphone with messaging tailored by the knowledge that the consumer has a twice a week cadence of going to the store and that she bought milk on Tuesday. Creepy, right? Chapter 9, "Collaboration and Integration Are Critical," and Chapter 10, "Mobile, Media, and Data—Oh My!," discuss more about how such creepy, and effective, mobile experiences are put together.

From Chief Marketing Officers (CMOs) of the largest brands, to small business owners, every marketer dreams of uncovering or tracking the optimal path to purchase for each segment of customers. Segmenting audiences and optimizing a path-to-purchase for each segment is almost impossible to orchestrate with today's technology and even the largest of marketing budgets. Where the sales funnel concept used to be a linear construct centered around the brand, today's mobile consumer has upended that model. The path to purchase might be traditional, moving from awareness to interest to decision to action (as Alec Baldwin so vividly illustrated in his famous sales speech in *Glengarry Glen Ross*), or it might be a direct path from an elevator conversation to an immediate iTunes download of a movie or book. The funnel has been irrevocably altered by consumers' ability to access all the available information about a product immediately upon hearing about the product, even if that interaction is in an elevator, not a showroom.

So how do we make sense of this new, collapsed funnel? The technology that so many marketers use today offers glimpses or "snapshots" of the purchase journey through dashboards and analytical tools that focus only on certain media or technology. A classic situation where this happens is with search marketing, where credit is given to the "last click," and the research path of the customer is not taken into account. When this happens, search (and Google, since it owns the majority of search behavior) often gets credit, but search might merely have been used as a utility—an expedient way for consumers to quickly connect with a brand they already knew they wanted to buy. Search gets the credit in many transactions, but the prime mover of a purchase might well have been an elevator conversation invisible to Google Analytics.

Nichole Kelly, author of *How to Measure Social Media* and CEO of Social Media Explorer describes the sales funnel as, "a really good model for visualization when you're trying to explain to someone who isn't a marketer or has more of a sales background, what the path you're trying to create to purchase looks like. I still use it as a model in ROI discussion all of the time because we're trying to explain that social, in particular, is a top of the funnel activity that disrupts the sales funnel in a good way, reaching people before they're ready to buy. However, when you actually track audience purchase behavior, where they're researching online, to which campaigns they're responding and what they're doing in social media versus email versus the mobile app, etcetera, the *funnel* begins to look much different. All of those different use patterns and activity start to look more like a neural network, in that there are hundreds of combinations and touch points that a company can have with a consumer that influence their purchase behavior that aren't being tracked today. If we could figure out the optimal path that creates the highest sales conversion rate, companies could probably double or triple their sales and greatly reduce their marketing spend, but we must analyze that path first."

For businesses, then, the data that matters isn't the "easy" data—the reductively linear, cookie-based trail from link to link, but the "dark matter" that lives offline, and in the hearts and minds of consumers. Increasingly, the technology that consumers use to bridge the gaps and connect offline recommendations with point-of-purchase price researching and other behaviors is a mobile device, and it is in syncing mobile behaviors with purchase behaviors that a richer understanding of today's consumer lies.

Indeed, our previous means of tracking ROI and attribution might not only be outdated now, they've probably been wrong for years. Kelly notes that "for decades, the cost per acquisition that companies have been measuring themselves against is inherently wrong because they have been tracking the last or first touch of sales attribution, while looking at all of the different touch points that a consumer or our buying audience has when they are actually making purchase decisions. If companies took the time to track that information and analyze what the actual purchase behavior is for each audience segment...the cost per acquisition that they are using today is three to four times lower than their true cost per acquisition. Because of this, they are crediting sales to those most obvious first or last touch points, and cutting marketing programs that are very influential in the buying process that are not the first or last touch. When they cut an influential element from their marketing mix because it ceases to show a return on investment, they end up shooting themselves in the foot because they didn't really know what was truly involved in the purchase process."

This cuts right to the heart of the arcane science that is media mix modeling—the science (or art) of determining the exact combination of media and messaging required to get your business's message across to consumers. If recommendations from friends, initially consulted via social networks, play a vital role in a consumer's interest in a brand and prepurchase research, "social" as a construct often gets left out of the attribution model because it is so difficult to tie to a purchase. But there is no question that social media messages, direct mail, and elevator conversations all play a role in driving online behavior—even when the first manifestation of that behavior is a search.

It's truly a far more complex model than traditional, reductive funnels can portray. Figure 3.2 shows an illustration Tim recently shared with a client, where he was able to have all stakeholders across separate marketing disciplines and responsibilities share what media or efforts were out in the market. As you can see through this example, the direct and indirect paths to purchase being monitored made for a messy and tangled maze.

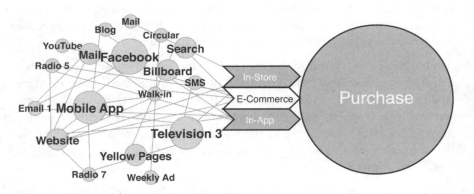

Figure 3.2 *Purchase attribution is a confusing path to follow or track, and seeing the last or first touch point as the greatest source of purchase influence or decision point may blind a marketer to what is indirectly contributing to sales.*

Companies have been plagued with a lack of technology and resources to implement or manage technology systems that accurately track customers and how they make purchase decisions. This is being somewhat cured by integration and collaboration, two things that social and mobile technology empowers. As Kelly states, "technology is improving with better analytics tools and marketing automation where we can now see many of the different activities in which customers are participating." Technology is beginning to reconcile customer behavior with the myriad ways that customers have to find and connect with brands; thus, we should see fewer marketers struggling to make sense of what in the noisy world of marketing is responsible for/contributing to sales, and fewer errors being made in modeling attribution. The excellent news for marketers is that with an increased convergence of social networking, search, discoverability, shopping, and payments occurring on smartphones, they should be able to draw connections between otherwise disparate channels and marketing touch points.

Commerce and Marketing Collide

Another fascinating and challenging attribute of today's flattened purchase journey is that marketers must now respect that their efforts are not going to always push a buyer down a path that the buyer doesn't already want to take. What this means for marketers is that a company and brand must be ready for the moment, the instant, and the impulse, when a prospective customer decides, thinks, searches, or is reminded to buy anything.

Smartphone owners are learning that they can quickly get to the information they need and want, when they need and want it—and businesses have an opportunity to provide an immediate path to purchase when the purchase decision is being researched. When it comes to shopping applications, we are still relatively early in the adoption cycle, yet already more than a growing minority of smartphone users rely on their mobile devices while shopping. This can lead to a better way for consumers to discover what is important to them *when they need it most*. In a matter of minutes, reviews and ratings can be read, or a point of purchase can be located either on a map or on a website through a browser or within a mobile application. When you consider how pervasive and universal this behavior will become, marketing must be ready for purchase consideration at every point in the purchase path.

While the abrupt reality of commerce happening everywhere can be seen as a threat to a company's traditional sales model, it can also be labeled a "commerce everywhere" opportunity for sales. Mobile commerce will increase through the proliferation of mobile shopping and the use of mobile wallet technology (discussed in Chapter 7, "Paying with Your Phone"), where companies will see an upward trend of customers who shop for and purchase goods and services with a smartphone or tablet. As of September 2013, many of the mobile applications installed and used on millions of smartphones and tablets are capable of making a purchase with merely the push of a button. These apps are teaching consumers that they can buy almost anything they desire, at almost any time and place where that desire happens. As the ability to buy is no longer limited by time or place, everyone in marketing must also wear a sales hat, as there are fewer boundaries between media, behavior, and purchase events. Nowhere will these events happen more than on smartphones and tablet computers over the next five years. Most companies will be required to reduce friction and barriers to these ubiquitous points of purchase, as consumers grow to expect it from everyone.

It's worth noting one other aspect of the mobile sales funnel. You might be thinking of mobile behavior as the actions a consumer takes while in a store or out of home. However, mobility is less about an out-of-home location than it is the ability to engage in commerce at the time and place of the consumer's choosing. Consider this recent research from Nielsen, which revealed that 95% of tablet shoppers and 72% of smartphone shoppers who make a purchase with their device do so at *home*.[4] Mobility in those instances isn't about the ability to research a purchase while in a store, it's the ability to react *instantly* to an advertising message on television, directly from the couch, before any other intervening actions. Mobility impacts the consumer journey from the desk to the couch, just as much as it impacts the journey from home to store.

Marketing, advertising, and public relations agencies will soon be held *more* accountable for driving the sales revenues for their clients. In addition to creative and strategic messaging, commerce capabilities will be woven into all owned digital media, such as websites, applications, interactive television, and digital out-of-home media. Publicis Groupe's Rishad Tobaccowala sees this as a great responsibility in the near future, stating, "Absolutely, commerce everywhere is already beginning to happen because in effect, people are integrating commerce into the entire marketing suite. The funnel has collapsed. Absolutely, the key thing really is not only about collaboration between sales and marketing, but it is increasingly about integrating commerce across the entire funnel."

When you think of all the ways that your business *could* integrate commerce opportunities at every mobile-enabled touch point, the mind boggles. Still, it can be difficult to conceive of all the possible ways that mobility can shortcut, and dramatically accelerate, the speed of consumer behavior changes. And nowhere is that more evident than in developing countries, as we see in the next chapter.

---

4. *A Mobile Shopper's Journey: From the Couch to the Store (and Back Again)*, Nielsen. http://www.nielsen.com/us/en/insights/news/2013/a-mobile-shoppers-journey--from-the-couch-to-the-store--and-back.html

4

Mobility and the Developing World

As innovation has accelerated over the past century, few successful technologies have disrupted business and economic structure globally. Yet mobile technology is doing this already on a wide scale, proving its power and unpredictability on an almost daily basis with new ways being discovered of managing, marketing, and operating business that did not exist before. Nowhere is this more evident than in developing nations, where the introduction of mobile commerce is increasing the pace of economic development and improving the quality of life, just as increased access to clean water or health care might. And if you are reading this from a "developed" nation, there are two lessons that we dive into in this chapter: first, that mobility accelerates commerce in dramatic ways—lessons that apply in any market—and, second, that mobility radically redraws the map of who you think your customers and suppliers could be.

We once could say that a "digital divide" existed between population segments with vast differences in their adoption of technology and access to the Internet. This was defined, and still is today, by income disparities and socioeconomic levels. There were the haves, those who could afford a newer computer and monthly Internet service, and the have-nots who were left behind because such devices and technology were unaffordable and out of reach.

In 2014, there are still valleys between socioeconomic groups and differences in advanced device ownership, media, and connectivity services they each may use. However, the breadth of this divide is slowly dissipating, and—in some cases—being erased with mobile phone and wireless Internet use. Smartphone usage and even mobile communications technology in general have caused enormous shifts in the economic prospects of people around the world. Mobility will certainly be seen as the most important technology-driven sociological shift in the last 50 years, because for the first time we can be connected and on an equal footing with anyone, all over the world.

Bridging the Digital Divide

And here is what mobile technology has really done for what we call "the developing world"—it's helping it *develop* in dramatic and rapid ways. According to a documentary[1] produced by Dr. Steven Shepard on some of Cisco's efforts to bring mobile Internet to previously off-the-grid areas in Costa Rica, the results are dramatic indeed. According to Shepard, a recent study by the World Economic Forum indicated that an increase in a country's mobile telephony penetration by 10% leads directly to a 2% increase in Gross Domestic Product (GDP), an increase in life expectancy of 15 months, and education for 600,000 children in that country. Pretty remarkable, eh?

Dr. Shepard also notes that access to the Internet enables local businesses in some of the most impoverished areas of Brazil to gain access to potential clients who might be wary of doing business with companies that are surrounded by poor living conditions. Thanks to the Internet, however, any business, no matter how remote or how humble its surroundings, can compete. Mobile telephony and mobile Internet access allow those entrepreneurs equal access, which results in an increase of money flowing in the direction of those underdeveloped areas—and a concomitant rise in the standard of living.

One of the most vivid examples Dr. Shepard cites, however, is the one that we would use to not only frame this chapter, but also draw a comparison between the

---

1. *The Network Effect*, 2011, produced by Dr. Steven Shepard, http://www.youtube.com/watch?v=1lUbyH2AOOg.

developing and developed worlds. One of the first instances where equal access to telephony had a direct economic impact was in the story of Almon Strowger, an undertaker who plied his trade in Kansas City, Missouri, in the 1890s. In those days, telephone calls could not be connected directly by the caller but had to go through an operator, and that operator had tremendous power. Strowger learned that the telephone operator was the wife of another, rival undertaker, and that calls placed asking her to connect callers to "the undertaker" naturally were sent through to her husband, not Strowger.

What Strowger realized near the turn of the twentieth century was the true impact of inequitable access to mobile. So he invented the automatic telephone exchange, or the Strowger Switch, to enable callers to connect themselves directly to the business or person of their choosing without an intermediary. The Strowger Switch was the principal enabler of unmediated telephone conversations for decades, and while it likely did wonders for Strowger's undertaking business, it had a much more profound impact.

The lesson of the Strowger Switch is this: Where technology removes barriers to information, economic development is jumpstarted. By enabling fair competition among undertakers (and presumably other businesses), the Strowger Switch enabled entrepreneurs to gain an equal footing, every bit as much as the tradespeople of the Brazilian slums Dr. Shepard illustrates in his documentary. Removing barriers to information has a direct impact on economic development and quality of life, and mobile telephony is powering the removal of those barriers all over the developing world, just as it did for Kansas City (and America) at the turn of the last century.

Today, mobile technology is inspiring similar stories, but as we already mentioned, those stories are really about behaviors and not technology. In the United States and across so much of the developed world, popular excitement is shared for the new functionality and gadgetry that has gone to market from manufacturers such as Apple, Blackberry, Samsung, and others. This excitement is valid, of course, as many of these new devices and the software that accompanies them (apps, cloud-based software, and services) further open and enable amazing applications that make life easier for those who own such devices. And while those applications make life easier for many folks who are living a relatively easy life, there is now an even greater effect in the developed world. Mobile devices are the "Strowger Switch" that empowers small businesses to better compete with large businesses, and consumers are more directly finding ways to save by cutting out retail and distributor middlemen.

Mobile commerce will drive tremendous shifts in economic structure for most of the world. It will put the power back into the hands of the individual, and connect buyers and sellers in ways that this planet has never seen. This is no exaggeration:

Mobile commerce has already played the role of economic democratizer with the enormous impact mobile banking (M-Banking) and mobile phone use has had in parts of Western Africa.

Consider that in Kenya, mobile technology is empowering widespread access to money and enabling small farmers with new ways to participate in and profit from larger agriculture markets that were previously all but inaccessible to them.

In 2007, Safaricom launched the m-banking enabler M-PESA in Kenya in partnership with Vodafone, the world's second largest telecommunications company. After its first full month of operations in April of that year, M-PESA had more than 52,000 customers. One year later, it had more than 1.6 million customers.[2] By April 2011, there were more than 14,000,000 M-PESA accounts believed to hold 40% of Kenya's savings.[3] What you can glean from this is that mobile technology made it dramatically easier for millions of Kenyans to save money, and that these changes happened with incredible speed. That dramatic shift to mobile savings—whether it was driven by people who used to save via other means, or simply from new savers, is evidence of the incredible behavior change that mobile technology facilitates. Today those 14,000,000+ M-PESA accounts are a visible artifact to a burgeoning new economic power and a sign of stability to other markets. And all this happened in a dramatically short period of time, thanks to mobility placing the power of savings directly into the hands of consumers.

The explosive use of mobile banking in Kenya is thought by many people to be the result of "need" instead of "want." Much of Kenya's population migrates from rural areas to urban centers where work is more widely available. Mobile banking enables these migrants to send money to family members back home, thereby distributing income on a more widespread basis, and M-PESA has been one of the greatest enablers of such services.

Susan Oguya, cofounder of MFarm, states, "Most individuals acknowledge the importance of the mobile-based banking service in a myriad of their daily activities. Usage patterns appear to be largely driven by personal missions and marketing strategies of service providers. Depending on the nature of activities and requisite levels of expediency users will employ M-banking in variable ways. Though mobile banking seems to cut across all groups, usage is more pronounced among younger age groups. With reference to income...we've seen that some users with no specific income sources were identified as regular users, implying a huge possibility that they rely on income of others. What this signifies is the fact that M-banking has created a formidable avenue for income redistribution."

---

2. Statistics from Safaricom's website.

3. "Vodafone," Wikipedia, http://en.wikipedia.org/wiki/Vodafone#Africa_and_the_Middle_East.

MFarm is a mobile marketplace and information provider that is helping more than 42,000 farmers and businesses reshape the agriculture markets. Farmers in certain regions of Kenya who are using MFarm for collective selling have reportedly been able to receive more than double the price for certain types of produce than when individually selling their produce through traditional means. Historically, these farmers were stuck with whatever price the nearest or incumbent broker would offer, as is the case with many agricultural supply chains around the world. While MFarm enables many of these farmers to directly connect with buyers, many who use the service have leveraged access to current market information and a transparent bargaining platform to use when selling individually to brokers or middlemen.

"Mobile banking provides hope for the unbanked," MFarm's Oguya stated in an interview with the authors. "The agricultural sector in many developing countries is characterized by a large number of small-scale farmers. Productivity is often low due to limited access to agricultural technologies. Much of the produce is consumed by the household while the remainder is sold to a few traders or on local markets. Among the obstacles to market participation, many farmers lack information about prices and demand in different markets and contacts to potential buyers. In recent years, mobile phone-enabled services such as MFarm have been developed to address these gaps and thereby facilitate market participation. Such services can be used to transmit market information (for example, on prices and buyers), connect buyers and sellers, or manage deliveries." On MFarm's future, Oguya states, "Our aims are to have East African farmers and other markets using MFarm to trade horticultural produce. This means that it will be a commodity exchange platform that will enhance traceability and transparency."

What we found fascinating about MFarm and M-PESA was how mobile technology tapped into a "hidden" market—the unbanked—and found ways to provide value for that market and tap into it to drive economic growth. These stories are not confined to developing markets. Here in the United States, Walmart has been able to make considerable inroads into the "unbanked" market by serving as a financial services provider for unbanked and underbanked individuals and families, with mobile deposits and electronic bill payment at the center of their offering. As mobile technologies directly connect customers with markets and remove intermediaries, the speed of economic development can increase whether the market is Kenya or Kansas City. But it is in the developing world that we truly see what enabling mobile commerce can truly do in a short period of time.

Simply connecting buyers and sellers and redistributing income stands to disrupt legacy economic and business systems around the world. This is a positive disruption that provides fairer access and opportunities to the individuals across traditional socioeconomic boundaries, while presenting huge opportunities for new and existing businesses previously not connected to a real-time market that now have the ability send and receive payments from almost anywhere. And as income redistributes, new markets open up to not only buy goods, but also to sell them.

The Holistic Impact of Mobile Technology

The true impact of mobile technology, however, is not simply in new markets and sales opportunities, though those are some of the more compelling stories. No, the true impact is in seeing how increased mobile penetration impacts *all* areas of business. Of the many people we have met who live in developing countries and who are experiencing the impact of mobile commerce, the majority went beyond sales and marketing case studies, and instead shared stories about improved operations and cost savings, from companies like these:

- A delivery company in Africa with 4,000 drivers who collect more than $400 billion in annual *cash* payments. Every month, the company asks a bank to help them find an alternative to cash for accepting card payments in the field, to which the bank responds, "Well, we can give you 4,000 fat bricks that allow card swipes and batch processing at day's end. That will cost you $8 million up front or we can rent them to you at a similar investment over time—now, you've got a viable alternative." Instead, that company has now outfitted drivers with a mobile point-of-sale (POS) unit using a low-cost Android smartphone that costs a fraction of the "brick" to operate. Money is moved instantly, with no more end-of-day batch processing, and drivers are now safer with cash transactions diminishing across the fleet to be replaced by card and mobile payments.

- A Kenyan company that sells a product to a set of distributors who then sell to resellers, and those resellers then sell to small shops that sell to the public. Currently, that company only knows what happens when selling to the distributors and loses sight of everything that happens to the product and its eventual journey to consumers fairly early in the overall sales cycle. But a mobile point-of-sale system company enables the entire distribution and sales chain and can move transactions from being predominately cash-based all the way along that value chain, to being based on electronic payments—which means they can see a flow of that data along the entire sales process, gaining some amazing insights.

For example, today the company does not know if all the brand advertising they are doing on billboards or other out-of-home advertising is having any kind of effect in Eastern Nairobi. By moving to a mobile point-of-sale, almost every transaction becomes fully traceable and tied to a location, so the company would know that a small shack near some of their advertising on Halie Selassie Avenue sold

50 units before 3:00 this afternoon and outperformed a similar retail outlet that was not proximate to outdoor advertising. This enables the company to optimize its marketing spend, sell more units, and redirect its expenditures more efficiently—which not only increases margins, but adds employment opportunities and further income redistribution.

There are countless ways that mobile commerce and mobile point-of-sale systems may improve business performance through operations efficiency and business intelligence. This is possible around the planet, but what is most remarkable about "going mobile" is that the developing world may surpass developed markets in terms of adoption and usage of such technology as there is less incumbent, existing technology already in place as there is in Western developed markets. Put simply, where there is no technology or little existing "wired" infrastructure, the intro-duction of wireless connectivity to web-based systems and information will more quickly be used.

The challenge in developed markets is that large incumbent organizations have a vested interest in not seeing disintermediation happen. In a market like Kenya, big banks and the big mobile network operators (MNO) will start this technological revolution, because they have little to lose and everything to gain. Kenya is starting from scratch with payment technology, whereas the United States, Great Britain, France, and Germany already have a near-universal install base of existing, non-mobile POS infrastructure, the current profitability of which is an impediment to converting to a mobile system.

For those developed markets, when small businesses are already paying $50 per month to rent equipment for accepting card payments, along with relatively high interchange fees to process each transaction, where is the incentive for the incum-bents to optimize? Here we can look to the developing world not as laggards but as vanguards for a new mobile-optimized payment system. One of the compa-nies leading these changes is Appconomy, which is building mobile commerce apps and services from their headquarters in both Shanghai, China and Austin, Texas. Appconomy's COO and SVP, Marketing and Business Development, Joe Canterbury, told the authors in an interview, "For some of these countries, China, India, Brazil and so many other emerging markets, it's been a total leap frog for the user and the retailers. Although the retailers have been around for ten years in those countries, they don't have decades and decades and decades of legacy sys-tems as Western markets do. So, it's much easier for them to leap frog into mobile commerce, so quickly. It's a huge trend—and it will get bigger. Be it POS systems, inventory systems, other enterprise systems, all of that is going to be changing fast at the hand of mobile."

As mobile commerce technology spreads in developing markets, the entire world will hear about it and learn from fantastic case studies that are emerging even as you read this. When you consider that there are countless areas of the world where geography and a lack of infrastructure prevent even a simple telephone line from connecting two people, it becomes logical to see how mobile technology can serve a necessity that was previously unknown.

We spoke with Steve Emecz, Senior Vice President, Business Development, EMEA + Asia Pacific for UK-based mobile payment company POWA, who referred to it this way: "[It's] evolution versus revolution. So, you'll see in certain markets, they will evolve more slowly—like in Europe. You'll see revolution in Latin American and in Africa because they don't have that fear of cannibalizing their existing base. I think it's very easy for us to look at the existing mobile footprint and the number of point-of-sale machines that are out there, and how much commerce is being done on mobile today and lose sight of the fact that you could have five, ten, even twenty times that in the emerging opportunity in the next two or three years in markets that, until now, have been held back by the capitalization requirements or infrastructure requirements—like electricity supply consistency, or mobile network availability for example. It is certainly a very exciting area."

The Mobile Accelerant

So here, ultimately, is what we hope you take from this chapter. First, mobile commerce is an incredible accelerant—whether it's introduced to Kenya or to a rural Walmart in a previously unbanked area. Second, the rapid development of previously underdeveloped economic areas will lead to new markets. In fact, the world's richest man as of this writing, Bill Gates, predicted in the most recent Gates Foundation Letter that "there will be almost no poor countries left in the world"[4] by 2035, which (hopefully!) is within our lifetime. When craftsmen who live in makeshift shipping containers in Costa Rica can compete on an equal footing with craftsmen in more developed communities and countries, income inequalities gradually start to equilibrate, and the standard of life for potentially billions of people improves.

What this means for you is that new markets for your products and services are opening up all over world, and in areas where you might not have expected to find your future customers. Of course, you could choose to ignore the impact of mobility on the developing world—but your competition might not. And the capital that increased access to the next India could be a strategic advantage for you, or for your competitors, for years to come.

---

4. Bill Gates, 2014 Gates Annual Letter, http://annualletter.gatesfoundation.org/.

5

Challenging the
Status Quo

Mobility is challenging the way commerce and business are conducted, and this is just the beginning. On August 15, 2013, the U.S. stock markets tumbled with drops in the Dow Industrial Average by 1.5%, the Standard & Poor's 500 by 1.4%, and the NASDAQ composite by 1.7%. Most media outlets and analysts issued the blame and pointed to poor earnings results and reduced performance forecasts issued on that day from two major big-box retailers, one of which is seen by many as a bellwether for the economy. Despite the release of several economic indicators that showed that jobs were being created and U.S. home sales were picking up, the markets continued to close each day at a loss for most of the remaining month. In the improving economy, customers were not necessarily buying less, but the markets might have been focused on the wrong retailers to gauge spending activity.

As the world goes wireless, contributing reasons for such missed expectations may lie in the fact that more consumers are able to find and purchase retail goods and services online and from the palm of their hand. In talking to hundreds of consumers while writing this book, that would certainly seem to be the case for many who are using Amazon to purchase items such as diapers, cleaning supplies, clothing, and food, instead of visiting a local retail or grocery store. The act of buying goods and services via the web or a mobile app matters just as much as the time and effort saved from not having to visit a store and stand in the checkout line. That is behavior change.

Change in business is imminent as there are ebbs and flows in society that constantly shift markets and economies. Plenty of contributing factors are at play in a large corporation's earnings report, revenue forecast, and share price. However, if you compared the Fortune 500 list from 2000 with the Fortune 500 a decade later, you would see that 40% of the companies on the 2000 list were no longer there in 2010. We are not stating that mobile technology is the lone or primary cause for such change. Mobility is certainly contributing to the changes businesses face today and the many new commerce pathways realized with apps, social networks, and other digital media are sure to disrupt legacy ways of conducting business.

Most companies see the world's population being armed with portable wireless Internet devices as a new opportunity for sales and marketing. But, there is another truth of mobility that should serve as both a stern warning to existing businesses and a beacon of hope for aspiring entrepreneurs and freelancers.

One thing the Internet has done since it became a part of the mainstream economy is to punish the middleman. The ability to access goods and services directly that previously required intermediaries has disrupted countless businesses from stockbrokers to travel agents. Mobile, however, is poised to be even more disruptive— especially if we consider mobility as a behavior more than just a mobile computing device.

We are entering a phase of commerce that some call the *Collaborative Economy*, a time in which peer-to-peer, disintermediated transactions and the sharing of consumables are beginning to become a more convenient and affordable way of shopping. AirBnB, for instance, has proven to be a disruptive force to the hospitality industry by creating a marketplace that matches people who need a room with people who have a room in a private home. While AirBnB may still be an intermediary aggregate marketplace for travelers, the means of moving the aggregation and merchandising of a particular market to the control of many providers and all consumers is what makes it so disruptive. This near-direct reality of one person connecting with other individuals or families, rather than only a few hotels or management companies, is already causing the hospitality and travel industries to rethink how to reach and convert travelers into customers. Already, many hotel chains who have enjoyed a frequent and repeat rhythm of guests over the past few decades may be finding that this new competition for attention and travel search traffic is stealing would-be guests.

What mobility adds to this equation is almost less important than what it removes—the need to plan ahead. Humans are creatures of impulse, and having the ability to call up goods and services in the moment of need, whenever and wherever we are, is absolutely going to disrupt businesses that do not have both a mobility strategy and more direct mobile channels to a market.

Consider this scenario: Imagine that you are working in your yard and discover that you need a hedge trimmer. You can immediately go to Facebook or send a text message to your neighbor and ask, "Can I borrow your hedge trimmer?" Well, imagine a near future in which the further morphing of Craigslist and similar systems get us to a point where we are never expected to own a hedge trimmer or a lawnmower. There might be one of each for every five houses so neighbors have a way to share in the cost. Let's call that fractional ownership, which now no longer needs to be restricted to things like timeshares and corporate jets. Who's going to suffer from this new way of doing things? Sears, Home Depot, Lowe's, and anyone else who sells things that lie dormant in our garages for most of the year.

In that sense, services like Uber, which allows mobile users to call up a town car, track the distance of that car to their location, rate their driver, and pay—all with a couple of taps on an app. All of this activity being tied to both your unique ID and a credit card—have the potential to be extremely disruptive. Certainly, there are the obvious disruptions: limo and taxi companies, for example. Of course, the taxi industry has responded with apps and services like Hailo and CMT's Ridelinq, and there is promise for the legacy business that innovation is not limited to start-ups. Think also about the companies that handle dispatching and payment for ride services—a mobile phone and a direct contact to Uber eliminates the need for a dispatcher, and also provides surety to an individual driver that he will, in fact, be paid, directly to his payment account, immediately upon completion of the ride. Mobile apps like Uber, then, will continue to disintermediate businesses as they eliminate the middleman existing between driver and rider. But the ramifications of Uber and its ilk go far deeper.

Functionally, what Uber provides is a nice ride, where and when you need it. Conceptually, however, it is more than that. It is fractional ownership of a limousine, at least as far as a user might care. Think about the reasons why you might own something—to be able to use it whenever you want—and consider just exactly what Uber represents: a threat to ownership, period. If your product or service can be "Uber'd," then your business better be the one doing the "Ubering," or the risk on your future profits might be too much to bear. The authors both live in urban areas (Austin and Boston) where a number of car and bike sharing services tied to mobile apps exist—Tim has been using such services in Austin since giving up owning a car in 2003, and Tom does not own a car in Boston. The ability to call up a ZipCar or Car2Go in an instant from a mobile app, places downside risk on a whole chain of companies connected to the automobile industry. In fact, we can even envision a day when an auto manufacturer doesn't sell a car to a person but deposits it in an urban parking garage tied to a satellite mobile unlocking and payment application, and it gets used 24 hours a day. How's *that* for disruption?

Certainly one of the most disruptive things about mobile technology is the ability it provides for one human to pay another human directly. In Boston, for example, we make extensive use of a mobile app called LevelUp, which allows customers to pay at the counter using their mobile phone, which is tied to a single credit card/payment account. Because the payment is handled through your unique account (and not simply by the swipe of a card), businesses that adopt this technology can offer LevelUp users individual incentives, discounts, and other loyalty benefits to encourage repeat purchases. It is easy to see the upside for a business here—but the downside risk lies in a less obvious place: with credit card companies themselves.

How LevelUp helps to enable the incentives that its merchant clients offer their customers is with the promise of lower fees for credit card transactions. LevelUp's *Interchange Zero* commitment states, "We've made it our mission to eliminate interchange." LevelUp batches payments—charging a whole bunch of them at once to customer cards—instead of charging one at a time. In doing so, LevelUp can offer businesses low transaction fees. Widespread use of this kind of service could reduce the number of transactions—and transaction fees—for legacy payment services. But that's not the only downside risk that this kind of disruption portends.

Consider the Austin-based company TabbedOut, a mobile payment and point-of-sale technology provider focused on the hospitality industry. TabbedOut essentially bypasses the point-of-sale systems currently being sold to restaurants and bars, providing both mobile payment and ordering systems without the need for dedicated hardware or infrastructure. What TabbedOut also offers businesses, thanks to the unique identifier of a mobile phone, is the ability to combine customer relationship management (CRM) and marketing capabilities all in one system, piggybacking on a device we all already have in our pocket.

When a customer pays with TabbedOut, businesses not only get paid efficiently, they also get valuable information about their customers—information that can be used directly to make the lives of their patrons better and increase loyalty. Think about how you feel when you enter your favorite bar, and the bartender has your favorite drink all ready for you before you even sit down. That's the promise of businesses that use technology like TabbedOut's point-of-sale system. In addition, a restaurant can make better, more relevant offers based on profile information tied to a mobile phone account. If you've previously ordered vegetarian food, a quick service restaurant can make tailored offers to you via mobile that don't try to sell you steaks.

As more businesses begin to embrace mobile payment services like LevelUp and TabbedOut, businesses that don't will begin to suffer several different kinds of pressure: differential transaction fees, perceived differential in customer service, efficiency, and marketing effectiveness. Over time, these pressures will combine and mount, making it difficult to compete in areas like the hospitality industry where there is already a high failure rate.

The other thing that startups like TabbedOut, Uber, and LevelUp highlight for businesses is one of the key drivers for mobility—the removal of friction from the transaction process. As consumers become more used to paying for things without even pulling out their wallets (or even their phone, thanks to contactless proximity signals from technologies such as Bluetooth Low-Energy and Near Field Communications), companies that *do* require them to go through multiple trans-action steps will suffer by comparison. Removing steps will become a competitive advantage, which results in a corresponding disadvantage for companies whose transaction processes seem more onerous by comparison.

We need look no further for proof than at the enormous impact Amazon has had on any number of businesses. Earlier in the book we discussed the concept of showrooming—the act of browsing for a product at a physical store, and then purchasing it elsewhere online. Amazon has made an artform out of this with its shopping and *PriceCheck* apps. The Amazon app essentially removes the need to type for a shopper to engage in showrooming. All you have to do is walk into a brick-and-mortar store, use your smartphone to scan the UPC code of a product you want, and Amazon thoughtfully adds it to your wish list or your shopping cart. As shown in Figures 5.1, 5.2, and 5.3, using Amazon's PriceCheck app gives you the immediate opportunity to scan the UPC code of a product and then order that product through an Amazon merchant, often at a lower price than the store around the corner.

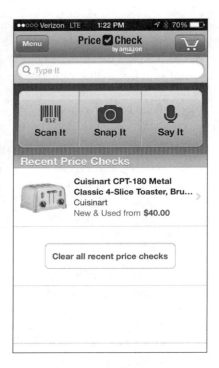

Figure 5.1   *The opening navigation for Amazon's PriceCheck application for iPhone. Note the four methods a user may use to search for an item: Type It, Scan It (UPC codes), Snap It (a photo), and Say It (with the user's voice).*

Figure 5.2   *The Amazon PriceCheck mobile application for iPhone performing a scan of a product's UPC code*

Figure 5.3 *The Amazon PriceCheck mobile application for iPhone displaying the search results for a UPC code scanned with the app*

In the early days of this behavior, it certainly had an impact on bookstores— Amazon's bread and butter (ask the former employees of Borders Books). However, Amazon has its sights set on far more than books, and numerous studies demonstrate the impact of Amazon on any number of big-box retailers. In fact, even your local supermarket may feel the effects of Amazon's mobile strategy.

Recently, Amazon introduced Amazon Dash, a small wand that connects to your home Wi-Fi network and allows you to scan common household items—and groceries—and automatically add them to a cart (or even a subscription, for commonly purchased items). No UPC code? No problem. Shoppers need only speak the name of the product into the Dash's built-in microphone, and speech recognition takes care of the rest. Again, this strategy is notable for what it removes—the need to write down a grocery list, remember to take that list, and go shopping. Instead, the moment you eat that last Klondike Bar—boom—another box is on the way.

Currently the Dash is tied to Amazon Fresh, which at the time of this writing is available in only a handful of markets. But there is no question that Amazon plans to go directly after the grocery business and any other local business that is not nimble enough to compete. Remember when Amazon invested in drone technology? Drones delivering books may have seemed a little far-fetched. Drones delivering frozen food before it thaws, however, seems not only plausible, but a genuine benefit.

While it remains to be seen whether the Dash (and Amazon Fresh) will be successful, it does highlight an important theme of this book. In a time when the mobile phone has become the ultimate convergence device, why would Amazon introduce a new device like the Dash? The answer lies in thinking, again, about a mobility strategy, and not simply a mobile phone strategy. The Dash is not tied to any desktop and does not require the user to pull out her phone and open an app; you simply pull it off your refrigerator door and scan your Cheetos. Mobility is all about removing the barriers between desire and commerce, between head and heart, and enabling transactions in the exact moment and setting that they are desired.

For the grocery industry, the downside of not having a mobility strategy could be enormous. Consider that grocers typically work with a margin of less than 2%. If businesses like Amazon Fresh, using the Dash, take even a small percentage of that business, grocers will have to adjust quickly to survive. To do so, they too will have to consider all that mobility implies. Supermarket shelves remain prime real estate, and one of the great landscapes for marketers to explore. A mobility strategy simply has to consider all the things a consumer might want to do while in the store as he gazes across this landscape and provide those services in a profitable and delightful way.

But make no mistake: even if a peripheral device such as Dash does not succeed, failure to embrace mobility could have disastrous results for nearly any local retailer. There are startups such as Instacart, Favor, and countless other mobile-first retail and grocery delivery solutions for consumers that may help sustain current customer business. These apps empower customers to play with their kids at the park while someone else does their grocery shopping, and also helps them avoid the +1 behavior of adding impulse and last-minute items to physical shopping carts. That may very well—and we expect it to—result in declining revenues for your grocery store.

Ultimately, all of media itself is being disrupted by mobile technology. As great department store merchant and U.S. Post Master General John Wanamaker once famously said, "Half the money I spend on advertising is wasted; the trouble is I don't know which half." The mobile phone and mobile technology are poised to create a significant downside risk for any medium (and certainly marketers, advertising, and marketing that use those media) that does not embrace mobile technology.

With a broadcast message, marketers know that they are reaching some portion of an audience, and that some portion of that portion will find the message relevant, but proving the effectiveness of those messages is a bit of an arcane art. Consider the two things that a mobile phone can give you: a unique identifier (not a computer "cookie," but a unique phone number that is likely being used solely by a unique human) and (for many mobile users) a discrete location.

As the convenience of mobile apps and services continues to entice users to trade personal information and access for those benefits, marketers will reach more of the exact people they want to reach in the exact settings or context in which their goods and services will be most relevant and attractive. This certainly presents significant downside risk for those goods and service providers that have not figured out the most optimal way to reach consumers; however, in a broader sense, mobility also presents a risk for traditional, advertising supported broadcast media and models in general.

Now, we are certainly not predicting the death of broadcast media; there will always be a place at the table for broadcast. But there will be significant pressure on broadcast platforms—from television and radio to direct mail—to match the efficiency and targeting capabilities that a unique mobile device offers, and the ramifications of that pressure are legion.

In short, the message of this chapter is that the dangers of not fully embracing mobility go far beyond a potential decline in web traffic for nonmobile-friendly websites (a problem that afflicts many restaurants, by the way). Failure to embrace the ramifications of what true mobility and in-the-moment, disintermediated transactions can mean for a variety of businesses can have enormous detrimental impacts on businesses and the ecosystems they inhabit. In most cases no one can predict how much. The upside of mobility and its positive changes brought to society are formidable; the downside and challenges to business, equally so. When you consider that, the conclusion is clear—standing still is no longer an option where mobile strategy is concerned.

6

Privacy, Trust, and Security

If you are running a company of any size and managing customer information, security is likely to be a key operational concern. Even for a small business that has only a small database of customers' email addresses, certain U.S. federal laws and informal rules of etiquette dictate how those email addresses may be used and/ or shared with third parties. And customers are beginning to be more cognizant of all the ways in which their data is warehoused and protected. Recent security and customer data breaches at retailers including Target and Neiman Marcus have made customers increasingly sensitive to sharing information and wary of how businesses are using their personal data. As communications and commerce converge on mobile devices, there is also added concern for protecting customers' personal and payment information required to facilitate business and relationship marketing via the mobile web and mobile applications.

Intimate Expectations

Assuring customers that their information is secure and kept private is one way to build more confidence, loyalty, and repeat purchases or referrals. Firms that can credibly make those assurances increasingly gain a competitive advantage. Related to this confidence are new marketing opportunities created by the popular belief that the smartphone is the most personal consumer electronic device that humanity has known, as substantiated by the unique qualities of intimacy and privacy that a smartphone provides to its user. The device goes to the bathroom with most users, a very private moment for some people, and we already highlighted studies that show that some smartphone users will answer a call, text, or social media notification during sex.

This intimacy can be observed on so many trains and busy streets where earphones protect the sounds from personal playlists and podcasts, while the small screen also empowers private viewing and reading content without the person sitting in the next seat knowing what media or message is consuming that moment of attention. Whether you consider mobile to be the second screen, or the first screen, one thing is demonstrably true: The mobile device is the most personal screen and provides a unique avenue for businesses to get up close and personal with their customers—as long as customers are comfortable with that level of intimacy.

Smartphone users are likely to become brand advocates through personalized content and an intimate brand relationship, as shown in Figure 6.1. This brand advocacy can produce referrals, influence purchases, and increase the likelihood of repeat purchases. There are also intangible motivators that resonate with smartphone users, such as feeling and being treated as an *insider* with exclusive access to non-public content and inside knowledge of a brand. The feeling of being involved with a brand, and having a one-to-one relationship with a brand or product will soon become a standard expectation from all customers.

As discussed in Chapter 16, "The Mobile Web," marketers now have the ability to segment mobile web traffic from desktop web traffic, and to serve up mobile-specific content that is more personal and relevant to smartphone users. You can keep mobile users connected...with content. Marketers must not necessarily feel stuck having to re-architect existing content to play on mobile or create new mobile-first content. Today's marketer can certainly capitalize on the lack of mobile content as an opportunity to deliver exclusives to mobile users (that is, non-public content) restricted to those registered and current customers or employ proven and intimate content delivery channels such as SMS "texting."

Between 2014 and 2020, mobile users will learn to expect personalized and contextually relevant marketing, messaging, and purchase opportunities at any time of day from wherever they are standing, sitting, or flying. This means knowing past purchase history, social media activity, and loyalty program engagement in addition to location, time of day, and scores of other insights from data that a brand may have archived/stored and the in-the-moment data that comes from users and devices. For all of this to happen, a number of diverse data systems and software must be reconciled, as discussed in Chapter 10, "Mobile, Media, and Data—Oh My!"

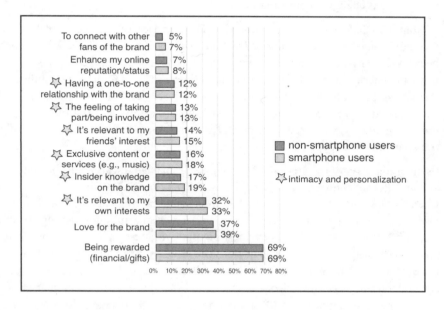

Figure 6.1   *What drives brand advocacy? Source: Global Web Index Wave 9 (Q1 2013) results. Mobile/smartphone users (N=1,183) smartphone users (N=1,682) were survey audiences.*

Building Trust

If a website or a mobile application is going to recognize an individual and her actions to lead her down the path to an informed and comfortable purchase, a high level of trust and confidence needs to be established between the individual, the brand, and the technology. This trust must go much deeper than providing security of the individual transaction—customers also must be reassured about the sanctity of data on their transactional history, lifecycle data, and other information that they have shared (even publicly) that can be linked to their account.

The effort to convince customers to pay at the counter with their phone or to buy something via that device from miles away may not be seen as such a foreign or even an entirely new proposition and may in fact help to accelerate that trust. Consider that for decades B2B businesses ("business-to-business," meaning businesses that sell to other businesses and not to individual consumers) have largely depended on paper checks to make and receive payments between each other. According to an Association of Financial Professionals Electronic Payment Survey, the percentage of B2B-related payments made by paper check went from 74% to 57% in the five-year period of 2007–2012. This is part of a larger digital trend occurring in the banking industry, and yet another example of how rapidly technology is changing consumer behavior.

In March 2005, Wells Fargo announced its Desktop Deposit service, available through Wells Fargo's *Commercial Electronic Office* (CEO) portal. Desktop Deposit helps Wells Fargo customers improve cash management by depositing checks from anywhere at any time without going to the bank as an effort to streamline the deposit process. By using the Desktop Deposit service, Wells Fargo business customers are empowered to improve cash flow and receive account information more quickly, while reducing costs, risks, and waste resulting from physically transporting check deposits.

In the initial days of the service, a bank customer needed a scanner, a computer, and an Internet connection to make deposits. This changed in November 2011, when *CEO Mobile Deposit* was launched to provide the efficiencies of Desktop Deposit and several unique capabilities to the bank's smartphone-carrying customers. This service has proven to be widely popular with customers across the United States, regardless of business type or size. The typical user of CEO Mobile Deposit is a business with a small number of high-dollar checks to deposit, with the average dollar amount per item deposited being $29,000. From the second quarter of 2011 to the second quarter of 2012, the number of checks deposited through CEO Mobile Deposit increased by 1,300%, and the dollar value of total monthly mobile deposits increased 700% in the same period. In 2012, $17B in additional wire transfer was processed via CEO Mobile, representing 150% year-over-year growth. As of March, 2014, businesses had deposited more than one billion dollars into the system.[1]

Such efficiencies and conveniences are also enjoying great success when extended to consumer and retail bank customers. In November 2012, *Wells Fargo Mobile Deposit* was nationally launched for the bank's retail customers. Using an Android or iPhone device, customers across the United States could easily deposit checks into their eligible Wells Fargo accounts by taking pictures of the front and back of the check. Today, Wells Fargo has 11.2 million mobile banking retail customers using the Wells Fargo mobile application or mobile-accessed website.

The volume of usage that Wells Fargo is realizing may not be surprising to some, as sharing personal information with a well-known bank that makes security

---

1. https://www.wellsfargo.com/press/2014/20140327_business-deposits-mobile-app

assurances each time you use their services may seem reasonable. When you consider the most popular tools and applications that U.S. mobile users have on their devices, from social media to banking to maps, there is little doubt that many other companies or organizations have access to certain details about users' lives, who may not have that level of trust. Trust is not implicit, and it must be derived from influences beyond the world of marketing for businesses to earn confidence from customers to reap the rewards of the mobile commerce revolution.

One such influence that may have rattled the confidence of many mobile users was the exposure of the United States National Security Agency's (NSA) data collection program known as PRISM (Planning Tool for Resource Integration, Synchronization, and Management). In May 2013, several media outlets reported unofficially leaked details of the PRISM program, including sharing of user information to the NSA from the most popular social networks, Internet service and email providers, managed network operators, and other consumer software companies. To many people, this news gave major pause for concern to know that the government had access to so much personal information, and all these breaches and leaks—whether from PRISM or Target—contribute to a general consumer unease with how much of their digital lives may not be secure from potential danger.

By region and country, trust and confidence is uniquely earned around the world as the perceptions of intimacy and personalization are steered by cultural and political forces that influence economies and societies. The empowerment and liberation brought to populations by mobility in some countries may be stifled in others by historic distrust of business and governments. One company seeing these differences firsthand is Appconomy, which operates a cloud-based platform for mobile marketing and commerce that directly connects consumers and merchants through its Jinjin marketplace and apps for smartphones, tablets, and feature phones, initially focusing on China and nearby markets. Appconomy's Joe Canterbury, who helped lead international expansion for brands such as Starbucks and Daimler, knows how comfort and confidence in sharing personal data on mobile devices differs around the world. He states, "Privacy concerns are such a bigger issue for individuals and for governments in Western Europe. There is so much more reluctance to share, so much more concern about people gathering information about you. Over there, you simply find an inherent kind of cynicism about the world...in China, [however],...I see much more of a willingness to adopt technology, to adopt new concepts, to adopt new brands, to accept that what works in other places can also work, especially if there's utility and cachet. Those are very different things. Utility always matters and cachet is always, particularly, important."

Canterbury adds, "For most Chinese, particularly the Chinese who are using smartphones day in, day out, this is the age of the China dream, and they have utter confidence where their life is and where things are going. They already have such a better life than their parents and they fully expect that their kids will. They are so confident and in many ways are very optimistic. That's not the case in places like Western Europe and the U.S. and Japan..." Canterbury adds that the Chinese are simply more comfortable communicating with their mobile devices than many other cultures where there is more of a cultural emphasis on direct personal communication and conflict resolution.

In this sense, privacy and security are as much about cultural sensitivities and differences as they are about technology. The amount of information people share—and their attitudes about the entities with which they share that information—varies across cultures. For a business to grapple with those differences, cultural awareness, authenticity, and ensuring that messaging is congruent across all channels (online and offline) are all part of earning and maintaining that trust.

Technical Concerns

When it comes to shopping or making payments with mobile devices, there are also as many technical concerns for privacy and data security as there are reasons to be confident in mobile transactions. From placing an order on a retailer's website while sitting in a coffee shop, to paying for dinner through a mobile payment system, there are a number of ways that infrastructure and security work together to build trust and confidence.

21CT provides an investigative data analytics and visualization solution called LYNXeon. LYNXeon fuses together disparate data, automatically determines behavioral links, and uses patented graph pattern matching to detect patterns that aid in network security, healthcare fraud detection, and criminal intelligence gathering. When it comes to the current most common and major threats to user data and payment information, 21CT's Vice President of Marketing, Kyle Flaherty, states, "Data breaches are the most common major threat, but the question is really about 'who' should we all consider the greatest threat. In that camp you see the full gamut of folks from malicious *hactivists* bent on hurting an organization's business, sophisticated criminal syndicates who are using the most advanced technology and methods to steal user data, or recreational and often bored programmers simply trying to get past a company's defenses. And in each case these folks are getting smarter, more organized, and in many cases well paid to do their work."

Many analysts believe that by 2015 more people will access the Internet through a mobile device than through a wired connection tethered to a desktop. Both companies and consumers must adopt good security habits to keep pace with this abrupt adoption of mobile computing, as the widespread use of 4G wireless devices such as smartphones and tablets also strains bandwidth and creates other challenges and security vulnerabilities. Flaherty explains, "Most notably you have the strain on bandwidth within an organization when users shift from their 4G and onto the corporate Wi-Fi, but that is the least of their worries. The main issue is this era of *BYOD* [Bring Your Own Device] and the vulnerabilities you then allow into your organization by allowing networked devices onto your corporate network."

"Imagine if you had a nicely secure bank," Flaherty continues, "with only one door in and one door out, a guard, and an alarm system. And then you decide to add a hundred windows around the bank...sure, it's nicer with all that natural light, but every window is now a vulnerability. It is a flawed analogy in our digital world, but you get the point when a major organization allows folks to get onto their network using their mobile devices/since they are now just allowing folks to collect internal data on their personal devices with no control of what happens after they leave the office. People are inherently lacking in intelligence around security in general and mobile security in particular. They are downloading mobile malware at a frenetic pace, and then logging onto the corporate Wi-Fi! Not to mention the simple threat of an employee pulling some sensitive data, throwing it in a personal cloud folder or file-sharing account so they can access it later without going through the VPN, and having that data stolen in a variety of other ways. It's all about the increase in the threat landscape and the daunting task of protecting it all."

There are also major challenges being brought to companies by misaligned network infrastructure, disparate systems, and technologies. Many CTOs and CIOs are still operating their businesses as if enterprise software takes care of itself. Flaherty states, "We know the folks that are stealing our data are smart, motivated, well funded, and aggressive. Yet enormous organizations are stuck in this medieval thought that a perimeter defense is going to stop it from happening. This is akin to the king who kept using moats and drawbridges after the advent of the catapult and ladders. The idea of a perimeter defense is still useful, but you need folks on your side going out and hunting down the bad guys already inside your network, and they are. It doesn't matter if they got in through mobile, although that is more likely today; the issue here is that we have to become more proactive, predictive, and preventive in our network security mentality."

As mobile payments and mobile wallet technologies go mainstream, there are additional concerns for the ways in which a mobile device connects to the Internet and cloud services to use a browser, use an app, or engage in a transaction. Flaherty explains, "The challenge in mobile payments is that you are now taking a physical + digital action and making it *all* digital, thus increasing the threat landscape unless you take additional security actions. Sitting in a restaurant that accepts mobile payments, I no longer have to hack the point-of-sale to then grab credit cards when they are swiped, I can do that, *plus* get on the Wi-Fi at the locale and start to ping all the mobile devices also connected and then identify all of those that happen to also house a mobile wallet. Granted, there are technologies on the phone that are being implemented to make this more difficult, but these are the same people who think moving their wallet from the rear pocket to the front made them more secure around pick-pockets. They are the same people that continue to use a four-digit security code to get into their iPhone. They are the same people that continue to make banking transactions over insecure Wi-Fi channels. Relying on the consumer to protect their own security may be the number one danger we face for mobile payment technology today."

Ultimately, the real promise of a mobile commerce journey won't be realized without consumers meeting us halfway and agreeing to share data. And they won't do that without assurances—in word and deed—from businesses that want to store and mine that data. And even with all the precautions that businesses can take, consumers are one weak password away from undoing all that effort. But what has driven much of the consumers' willingness to share sensitive data via mobile is the promise and convenience of mobile payment systems, and that's exactly what the next chapter focuses on.

7

Paying with Your Phone

In talking with dozens of merchants about their expectations for mobile marketing and mobile commerce, we asked questions about how their expectations for both communicating with and transacting with customers have been altered by mobile technology. Many of these businesses used mobile payment systems and many more did not. Not one of them started off saying, "I wish my customers had more ways to pay with their phone."

Instead, we heard questions from confused business owners and managers such as

- "How does mobile help me get more people in my store?"

- "What's different about my mobile website that would have more people try us out that have never been here before?"

- "I am posting deals to social networks and our blog. How do I know if that is driving traffic to my business, and to which location?"

- "We significantly invest in search marketing. How am I sure that is paying off in sales?"

- "How do I learn who my best customers are? I have no idea who they are. And, how do I get those customers to bring their friends?"

- "I don't know why, but we have always had a billboard out on the highway. How do I measure what it is doing to drive business?"
- "We email deals and post offers to social media, and I am placing ads or coupons in the newspaper, but none of these things actually talk to each other, so I have no idea how they work together, or how each of those efforts works alone. They are each in silos on their own, so I often see them as kind of useless to me."

If you have been in marketing over the past decade, many of these questions and challenges may sound familiar, and you may already be successful in addressing a few of them. Even so, you can be confident that almost no business has mastered all these issues. Unless you have a company culture that allows for consistent collaboration between business processes and departments, it is most likely that solving many of the preceding business riddles has been too broad to address or conquer. That is, until now: Mobile technology is fast bringing new ways to reconcile transaction data with media attribution and other paths to purchase.

While few marketing challenges revealed by businesses are about commerce in the traditional sense of a money transaction, the value of a transaction does help define the relationship between a business and customer. When someone pays for something, the exchange of money is the easiest part. The fact that it is easy is also part of the market ignorance from which businesses suffer today. That fundamental connection between a buyer and seller now has multiple brokers and middlemen who've eroded that trust-building moment when money is physically or digitally exchanged. Merchant technology, payment processing, banks, and other players have distorted the view that businesses may have of their customers. Payment technology that is now carried in the hand of a customer as much as in the systems of business also stands to reduce the friction and perceived distance between those two parties.

Mobile Wallets

Many people have a Utopian-like vision of the near future where we can walk around with only a mobile device in our pocket, leaving our wallet at home or altogether replacing our physical wallets with a digital version that lives on a mobile device. Today, except for a driver's license and other government-issued identification cards, it is possible to have a usable copy of plastic cards used as confirmation of organizational membership, loyalty, insurance, and credit and debit payments saved in a mobile wallet application. This inherently would make both one's life and pockets a little less heavy.

This is all made possible in many different ways. In addition to the conveniences that mobile wallet technology brings to users, even more efficiencies may be realized by brick-and-mortar stores, service companies, and more.

People exchange value, and not just monetary value, as customer service and conversation are mixed with the goods bought and sold. It is more difficult to gain insights at scale for multiple reasons. Most point-of-sale (POS) systems in use today are meant only to transact and ring things up. They are not customer systems; they are sales systems. For the majority of businesses today, cash is exchanged or a card is swiped, and the deal is done with little to nothing recorded against the transaction related to the qualitative conditions of the sale or the customer's desires and disposition.

A restaurant, for example, may want to look past transactional data into what was bought at what time on what day of the week, reconciled with the fact that a "four top" (party of four) was seated at a table and a ticket was opened up at 6:09 p.m. Then at 6:24 p.m. that table ordered a specific soft drink and a glass of a specific wine brand/varietal. At 6:56 p.m., the appetizer order for calamari was sent to the kitchen. On top of all this, did someone at the table check in with Foursquare, or do they already like us on Facebook? Understanding those sequences and details can help build a meaningful relationship between the restaurant and its customers. If a mobile payment app (brand-issued or mobile wallet) is used by someone in that group of four to settle the evening's bill, it may present a great opportunity for the restaurant to know much of this information about that individual and improve business performance. A server might suggest a related drink or menu item to them on a return visit, and there are opportunities to improve promotional results (coupons, email, and social media) to drive incremental visits and perhaps even make inventory control more efficient.

For today's ideal reconciliation of purchase and data insights to be analyzed and work together as just described, there is an essential need to integrate certain systems and information to give a business a clear and actionable view of its customers. As illustrated in Figure 7.1, a simple integration is possible with a minority of POS systems that involve multiple systems and data sets.

While writing this book, we explored hundreds of businesses that accepted mobile payments through brand-issued, banking, and universal mobile wallet applications. The ease of use of several apps, along with simple utilities emerging that allow preordering meals or participation in a loyalty/rewards program, demonstrate that many brands are already leveraging transactions with customer insights and preferences. A few examples are shown in Figures 7.2 and 7.3.

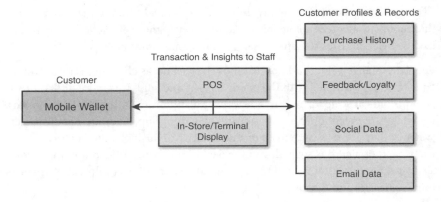

Figure 7.1   *How a business may integrate customer data with a POS data platform being the center of certain customer information and purchase data, whereby inbound activity data is recorded within specific customer profiles or customer groups/segments, and while insights and content direction help steer outbound and "push" communications in owned and paid media efforts.*

Figure 7.2   *Screenshot of Tim's Starbucks card on the Starbucks iPhone application. Note Pick of the Week where free apps and Apple iTunes downloads can be found, as well as the location-based notifications for where stars (denoting the various loyalty tiers) are earned.*

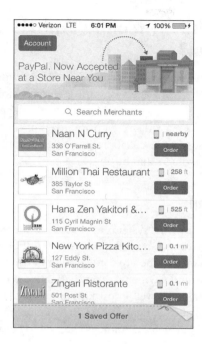

Figure 7.3 *Screenshot of the PayPal iPhone wallet application, which incorporates an Order function alongside the ease of sending payments as simple as addressing an email address.*

There are responsibilities for convincing people to pay with a mobile wallet or payment service. A business that incorporates such services must make the process either easier or much simpler for customers than taking a credit/debit card out of their pocket and swiping a payment into a POS terminal or cash register. In Canada, most of Europe, and soon in the United States, there is also a secure option to use a credit or debit card with a chip and pin technology known as EMV (for the founding consortium of Europay, MasterCard, and Visa). Mobile wallet and contactless payment systems offer the promise of removing friction from the moment of payment. That is what wireless computing has done already in removing and replacing steps from existing processes and systems, while providing tangible benefits to both the customer and the merchant. Even technologists and marketers who have hailed the arrival of Near-Field Communications (NFC) technology as the harbinger of widespread mobile payment use agree, often saying "It has to be easier than using my credit card." It is not as simple as that, however.

What Will It Take for Mobile Wallets to Be Successful?

So, if simply making our pockets lighter by digitizing payments and eliminating weighty items in our physical wallets isn't great enough motivation to have throngs of people using this technology, what will it take? Interdependent on one another, the three key influences that will lead a critical mass of consumers to consistently use a mobile wallet will be open collaboration, sustained education, and use benefits that serve both customers and business.

Open Collaboration

For mobile wallet and payment systems to succeed in the majority of North America and Europe, strong partnerships must be built on the premise of open software collaboration and cooperative integration of diverse technological systems and platforms. Several payments executives interviewed for this book stated that even the largest and most well-known brand name that seems to have all the pieces of the model (large existing user base, substantial investment, and fully integrated into POS or payment technology) has yet to be successful. Yet consumers will hardly use such innovative methods of payment if they do not allow for existing payment technologies or until the physical act of using a mobile payment method requires less effort than using a plastic credit or debit card. There is also the need by retailers to leverage business data and marketing intelligence platforms that may be integrated or used alongside payment technology. A great example of a brand succeeding today is Starbucks, a company now seeing more than 30% of its U.S. transactions, or 10 million per week, coming from payments made using the Starbucks mobile application, according to its Q4 2013 earnings call, while still accepting traditional cash, credit, and debit card payments in stores. Such integration and alternative options are necessary to make overall systems more efficient, less costly, and to leave open the opportunity for customers to have a choice in what they use to make payments.

"We know that as powerful as our technology is and the fact that we've already been able to introduce LevelUp to five thousand merchants and one million users, we still have a long way to go to be a ubiquitous payment solution, anywhere our customer goes. Our belief is that the only way to get there is to be an open platform. That means developing partnerships, some of which are public like you've seen with our partnership with [the POS system] Aloha, and some of them are behind the scenes, but all of them are taking advantage of our open platform, to build upon the right relationships that meet the operations and technology needs of merchants," states Andy Freedman, former VP of Strategy and Revenue at

LevelUp, a mobile payments solution for business and consumers, whom we interviewed for this book.

When speaking with merchants, most of them stated that they would love to have everybody use the same payment method, with lower fees on transactions. Lower fee (payment exchanges, transaction-related charges) advantages accompany most new POS and mobile payment solutions coming to market now, and even the smallest businesses see the opportunity to save thousands of dollars per year. Many of those systems are being introduced to merchants with unique integration requirements, training programs, and special fees that also have many businesses that stick to what they have in place today and have used for years. This is not a situation of old versus new as much as it is an effort to protect both existing and future revenue opportunities held by incumbents and new market entrants who each have certain value to merchants today. For merchants to accept all forms of payment, including mobile wallet transactions, a more cooperative effort must be put forth by the payment solutions companies that align technologies to work within the same business framework of hardware, staffing, and service cost control.

Education

As with all new and innovative technologies that come to market, there is often a steep learning curve for users targeted to adopt the new technology and regularly use it. The businesses and organizations that make the initial moves to capitalize on that technology should play the lead role in making customers aware of it while instructing customers on how to use it. This need for education is paramount in achieving both critical adoption by customers and consistent awareness by the front line of a business that can help drive adoption and subsequent greater sales and cost savings. Several times we have been able to find a coffee shop using a mobile wallet's nearby business locator, walk up to the cash register, and offer to pay for an order with that service, only to have a blank stare meet us from across the counter. Any business that wants to convert more customers to mobile payments through a smartphone or tablet application must be instructional, almost holding the hands of customers—and staff—through the initial months or years.

Rick Orr, founder of TabbedOut, a POS-integrated mobile payment solution for the hospitality industry, explains how a bar in Delaware is making its customers aware of the new way to pay and seeing phenomenal adoption. "We were shocked by their tab volume the first week they started using TabbedOut," noted Orr, who went on to note that they would see hundreds of TabbedOut transactions in a weekend from this particular bar, which is in a remote market where TabbedOut doesn't really promote their solution. The bar had made a display demonstrating the number of credit cards left at the bar by forgetful patrons and prompting their customers to use TabbedOut to avoid making the same mistake.

Certainly there are creative ways to educate customers and maintain awareness of changes a business may make to its purchase or payment capabilities. Through social media, email, direct mail, television, radio, and onsite education, any business can create a change in the way business is conducted. This is also a fantastic opportunity for marketing departments and agencies to provide training communications to staff and customers. Although *going mobile* is a natural and evolutionary behavioral change for society, it is still just that, a behavioral change. Consider the opportunities your business has to train everyone involved to use technology in a way that results in more efficient operations and personalized experiences.

Use Benefits

As part of educating both merchants and consumers about how they may respectively sell and buy things with mobile payment technology, there is also an urgent need for *everyone involved in transactions to look beyond the transaction* for the true benefits of mobile commerce. Many mobile payment and wallet solutions incorporate marketing analytics and business intelligence as part of the solution. As described earlier, connected technologies, including a store's POS, CRM, and/or loyalty program with shared personal information from customers, can result in great things. TabbedOut's Orr adds that the bars that use TabbedOut know that volume and revenue depend on efficiency, and they recognized the benefit of TabbedOut from the beginning. Understanding that benefit motivated the bars to initiate their own ways to inform customers that this is how they prefer to be paid. Bars that use TabbedOut successfully also see it pays off for the staff. The average tip given by TabbedOut customers across the U.S. is close to 23%.

TabbedOut and many others in the mobile payments space also provide marketing analytics to their customers. This a general trend across marketing and operations today, with social and mobile technology empowering businesses with the ability to merge transaction and profile data and learn more about what the people paying are doing. Across all industries, businesses stand to benefit from the move up the data stream from the payment alone to the transaction, including customer information and conditions that surround that transaction.

With the convergence of life on a smartphone that may know a person's location, communication routines, and preferences by brand and time of day, the last mile for many businesses is tying all the above to purchases: purchase attribution, coupled with the ability to frame the context of the situation, events leading up to and following the purchase, alongside endless access to other data about conditions of the day and other factors. To put it more succinctly, consistent use of certain apps and cloud-based technology on a device that accompanies its owner everywhere may help a business deliver relevant and meaningful experiences to customers unlike anything humanity has previously known. A combination of the mobile device itself and the big data that accompanies use of that device presents huge potential to reduce friction and simplify the buying process. Consider the information and insights you may collect as people walk into your business and buy things there or through e-commerce. Now a business can understand who its customers are in the real world, including their social personalities from data either publicly available or voluntarily provided. You can bind those two data streams together and execute individual and personalized ways to reach out on a person-by-person basis.

Beyond the transactional utility of mobile apps and mobile wallets is the promise that all businesses can forge close relationships with customers. Shopping has changed over the past decade with e-commerce, forcing many retailers to extend or move their catalogs and merchandising to a digital presence. Many consumers have already stopped stepping into their cars or walking into a store to shop, as there is an easier and simpler way to shop online. The way customers pay for services and buy goods is the next big shift in commerce: The convenience and portability of mobile devices, especially smartphones, will increasingly drive an expectation that all businesses be mobile-ready in terms of payments.

8

The Slow Road to Mobile Commerce

No one can doubt that it is a challenge to keep up with the weekly, often daily, announcements and press releases about new products and technology being launched. In fact, it can be fascinating to see how entrepreneurs, developers, and investors are pouring efforts into being the first to market with even the most outrageous ideas for the future of humanity. Various forces also are at work that govern a company's speed of adopting mobile technology and further what it takes to reach, convert, and sustain mobile users as customers. In some cases, businesses are even trying to actively convert their existing customers into mobile users.

We expect 2015 to likely be a breakout year for media and transactional commerce to come together, as so much of consumer attention and media focus is literally squeezed by the small screen of smartphones and figuratively handicapped by the collapsing purchase journey funnel. Mobile users are growing to expect a digital experience as smart as the device on which it is experienced, and marketers are under immense pressure to increasingly be accountable for revenue production from their media, advertising, and communications expenditures.

And while businesses will enjoy multiple new opportunities with mobility to drive this revenue, there will still be hesitancy on the part of agencies and brands to invest in these new and more efficient technologies that make mobile commerce possible.

The Denial Problem

Throughout 2013 and 2014, it was—unfortunately—commonplace to hear a company executive dismiss the need for or express unwillingness to incorporate mobile strategy and tactics into their marketing or customer service mix. It wasn't surprising to hear statements such as, "We don't know that mobile is worth the investment," or "I don't really think our customers use mobile." Many times these companies believe there is a certain merit to such statements because they either have recently invested in other (legacy) technologies or they simply have not seen any business slipping away from them...yet. It is the former of those two situations that delivers the greatest challenge to large brands and enterprise business, and it may be that too many businesses are simply afraid or ignorant—or both—of the urgency of going mobile.

The issue of desktop blindness is also a great contributor to denial on the part of many business owners and executives who fail to see or observe customer behavior from their desks and office windows. Often, when a business finally realizes that its most influential customers are gravitating to a competitor that has a more efficient mobile discovery, shopping, and buying experience, it is too late to catch up. This is already happening in metropolitan areas, where certain ride-sharing mobile apps are enabling commuters to circumvent established mass transit and tax systems that have not extended booking services via a mobile app or website. The threat of being late to market should diminish sometime between 2016 and 2017, as technologies become much easier to implement at lower price points, thus empowering a faster speed-to-market.

Still, if you own a business or if you are in a marketing oversight role, now is the time that a mobile-friendly (or responsive) website and blog and perhaps a mobile application or text-messaging program can help you capitalize on the behavioral shifts happening due to smartphone use. You can learn from what a small investment tells you today in terms of data, analysis, and observations of behavior. We do not offer such general direction to a client or reader of this book as a "build it and they will use it" suggestion, yet we can tell everyone across any industry that mobility is already impacting their business, as discussed in Chapter 5, "Challenging the Status Quo."

It may take convincing, but there are some marketers who have moved early to grasp and leverage mobile. Those who have invested in mobile technology may have seen the results of acquiring and retaining customers and increased sales directly correlated to mobile. It is also hard to dispute observed behavior, as when retail marketers walk around their stores and see shoppers on their phones. This often becomes an "aha moment." Of course, to build consistent use of new technology and to change behavior, you have to start small and invest wisely. Rebecca Roose with MyWebGrocer, a leading provider of e-commerce and e-marketing solutions to the grocery and consumer packaged goods industries, has experience with such rollouts. She states in an interview with the authors, "There is always a mix of our clients that is willing to try new tactics and technology and those clients that tend to be more conservative, preferring to see proven ROI or demonstrated use by their peers. The keys to the adoption of any new technology or tactic is identifying and succeeding with early adopters and then demonstrating these successes to build confidence among mass adopters."

Many marketers today also deal with executive leadership in their organization that—either out of natural ignorance, denial, fear, or a combination of those things—is not leaning into mobility and is simply not sure about the next direction in which they need to move. This is fair, as leadership must understand that this is about consolidating and integrating systems rather than what has historically happened: integrating technology into a business for the past 20 years by just dropping the new on top of the old, legacy upon legacy. With mobile, however, the added layer of how humans are changing the ways in which they transact using mobile commerce means that the latter kind of integration is destined to fail, or at least fail to take advantage of all that mobility can offer.

The Engineering Problem

While talking to businesses that have not made an investment in mobile assets or purchase points, we found many enterprise organizations in the same situation, dealing with uncertainty and struggling to understand what the order of the day should be from a technology standpoint.

It used to be that when a group of engineers was commissioned to build something, they would often succeed in delivering a product or service that thrived in its own environment but did not need to integrate with or play well alongside incumbent technologies and business processes. As some of the more intuitive and user-friendly tablet POS systems that also accept mobile payments are being implemented by small businesses, people using them may find that new and additional mobile wallet applications will not integrate or be accepted into their new investments. Too many times we have heard statements such as, "There is no API for our new POS system, so we can't make it work with anything"; "It's yet another closed ecosystem"; "It's a walled garden, just like our old POS system." On the other hand, there are open-source POS systems that integrate with other payments and customer information systems, yet most lack consistent support. The challenge with POS systems today revolves around the fact that the industry lives in a two-step distribution channel model, much like Dell stepped into the personal computer world, circumvented the middleman, and sold directly to consumers and business. That means, until mobile POS technology becomes more prevalent, dealers can simply walk into a business, look at the current POS system, and offer support services such as backup, changing the tape in the printer, and recovery from virus attacks. These dealers are locking many businesses into outdated legacy POS systems by simply providing such services, and most of the retail world is still in that model.

As in any established market reaping profits from existing technology, there are challenges to fully disrupting that market. It will take either a well-funded and growing mobile network operator (MNO, such as AT&T, Verizon Wireless, Vodafone, or Rogers Communications) or a well-funded and growing bank to break that status quo and explode into the POS market to standardize it. Still in 2014, the growing number of tablet POS systems such as ShopKeep, that also effortlessly integrate mobile payment methods like PayPal, stands to force market changes without waiting for incumbent players to move first.

The Expense Problem

Most of the existing payment and operations technology in place today was budgeted and bought a decade or more ago. Many CTOs cannot get out of their heads that, "Ten years ago, we spent $30,000 on that server back there, and these four terminals that sit on the counter, and I paid that money." Perhaps they are even still making lease payments on it. They go on to state something such as, "And then it took forever for the system to talk to the accounting system, to send QuickBooks the daily stuff, then to send to the inventory management system, so what else does it need to talk to?" They often fall back on the argument that they made a huge investment in the past and, "If it still works, why would I need to replace it?" It does not matter that the system may be running Microsoft Windows XP without Service Pack 1, and they do not seem to care that that machine has not been rebooted in four years. The investments associated with making new technology work with such older systems have most business owners thinking the same will be true with mobile technology. However, this changes with the mobile commerce revolution, with new systems being competitively priced to implement with existing POS, revenue management, and customer service systems. That is the only way the incumbent players can figure out to monetize the mobile revolution.

Businesses must go further than integration, where old technology is replaced with new systems and hardware. The truth is that mobile technology can deliver certain operating efficiencies, removing steps and friction from incumbent processes. It also has the potentially unintended consequence for a business of reducing operating expenses through reducing headcount needed for certain operations. For instance, a hotel may reduce the number of people needed in the lobby or at the registration desk because guests are able to check into the hotel and open their room doors with nothing more than a mobile device, such as a smartphone. This is a distinct business advantage to new wireless and smart mobile technologies.

The Patent Problem

The ugliest challenge to mobile commerce proliferation is that there are squatters in the industry that hold patents on mobile payments and mobile ordering. All you have to do is search for lawsuits against GrubHub, Apple's Passbook, and the Starbucks Mobile App. This should only be a short-term problem for the most promising innovators in this space, as history has shown that similar business revolutions sort out such conflicts and disputes. Some innovators will get crushed immediately or eventually run out of business, but often the final product is reduced to what is really unique about a technology solution, and more (hopefully) reasonable license fees ensue.

To be blunt: If you are a startup, you do not have two years to wait things out. You need business and customer traction now, or yesterday. The intellectual property issues in play are nothing to ignore, and it is critical to be diligent with patent research before too much is invested in any one direction of developing a new technology. Related, the United States patent system may keep so much of the promising technology from being adopted at scale, and that speaks to the super-litigious history of the country. Until this is reformed, it may kill innovation around mobile payments for the foreseeable future.

Who Will Lead or Follow?

Ultimately, we are still at the cusp of a shift. When it comes to mobile payments, it has been witnessed with Google Wallet that it is not easy for a new technology innovation to achieve mass use, even from a powerful industry player such as Google that has previously been successful with immediate, sweeping changes. Put simply, there are too many entrenched players in the broader payments industry that will not allow for any new breakthrough to quickly disrupt the existing ecosystem. Mobile payments likely will not suddenly disrupt or replace any existing alternate forms of payments, such as credit cards or automatic clearing houses (ACH).

Another way to understand how difficult it will be for any one company to run away with the mobile payment business is to consider today's competitive set of players. Picture walking up to a store—most storefronts have three to five stickers in their window to let you know that they accept Visa and MasterCard, maybe

Discover and American Express. Now you have an audience converting over to using PayPal, Isis, or Google Wallet. And the idea is that businesses, especially small businesses, want to be able to accept anyone's money. Therein lies a major challenge to closed POS systems, as there is no clear and simple path to a day where no one is carrying plastic.

Still, transactions will be increasingly executed via mobile as mobile payments are slowly considered mainstream. One disruptive force that may accelerate adoption of mobile commerce is political campaign cycles. This may have a substantial effect in 2014, and it will certainly have a big effect in 2016. The 2012 campaigns made effective use of fundraising via mobile email, mobile messaging, mobile websites, and mobile apps. With so much money at stake in the next series of campaigns, the use of these tactics will increase as immediacy and direct connection to voters is attractive to campaigners and fundraisers.

Finally, frequent announcements from equipment and hardware manufacturers give stories to the press and early adopters that promise the world will finally have a universal standard for executing mobile payments—contactless and otherwise. However, the mere velocity of such innovation, where something new is launched almost weekly, makes the hope for anything to be as standard as a magnetic stripe on a card (or the paper check before it) unlikely for any venture capitalist or entrepreneur to anticipate.

Quiet Confidence

Of course, so much of what is possible is not always plausible. An enormous amount of work still needs to be done for brands to have assets such as location-aware websites, and for those sites and mobile apps to start to leverage the existing data that medium-sized business to enterprise brands have stored in enormous email or customer databases. Businesses will find this challenging if, for instance, they still have a direct mail database and a separate email database, neither of which is reconciled in a central customer relationship management (CRM) system.

Consider the value of location. With digital assets today, brands have the capability to know a user's location with greater accuracy all the time, not always dependent on GPS coordinates. There is also the increasing opportunity through IP addresses to know someone's location when she uses a mobile app or clicks through an email. That gives a brand the opportunity to deliver something more relevant and personalized, increasing the propensity for users to click through the ad, search the results, or take some other type of action, whether that is just subscribing to an email list or finding directions to the store. It could mean downloading a coupon to use at the store or simply influencing a store visit, whether an on-device purchase or luring them to a physical point of purchase. The point is, there is tremendous innovation out there, and major brands still are far behind because they have not yet optimized what is already available in terms of known data.

We did not see a big technology breakthrough in mobile commerce in 2014, and for good reason. What will more likely propel mobile commerce forward is the quiet confidence that is incrementally building every day with consumers. Mobile commerce will become synonymous with digital commerce, and, eventually, just commerce. We have seen this already with mobile in general beyond commerce, where mobile experiences have begun to rival or exceed the importance of traditional desktop experiences for many companies and domains.

Most retailers and brands have established a significant presence in promotion and loyalty programs, and some have even made great strides in mobile; however, most of them have a long way to go to truly maximize the effectiveness of their mobile initiatives. Ultimately, this is the source of the conflict at the heart of this chapter— while mass adoption of mobile technology is happening now, standards around mobile payment technologies and related systems are not proceeding at the same pace. The day will come very soon, however, when businesses and customers will all get to the finish line at the same time, and the floodgates for mobile payments and mobile-enabled services will open.

9

Collaboration and Integration Are Critical

The term integrated marketing *has been around for decades. For many marketers and business owners, this term simply means a concern for brand alignment and media scheduling: that is, the message is the same online and offline, things look the same, the colors match, and so on. Integrated marketing campaigns have historically been planned on Gantt charts for messaging, scheduling the various forms of marketing from direct mail to television to fire in succession and in support of each other and of a campaign.*

There was indeed a time when integrated communications experts could strategically plan the sequence and delivery of the messages that made up a campaign. The Internet, however, disrupted this practice just as thoroughly as it has so many other fields. While many organizations continue to be successful in planning the sequence of advertising and marketing messages over a plethora of channels, the idea of combining multiple creative and media disciplines as an aligned force of service has become more difficult with the explosive consumer use of cable television, the World Wide Web, digital video recorders (DVRs), satellite radio, and social media.

The arrival of such widely accessible services and the splintering of media that accompanies them shifted the control of information and delivery of entertainment content largely into the hands of individual users, not companies. Mobile broadband and the widespread use of smartphones are now creating a new layer of segmentation to this marketing media puzzle, while also introducing new advantages to businesses and agencies that combine media and technology systems.

As Brad Mays, general manager of Edelman Digital in Chicago, told the authors in an interview, "it's time to change *mobile* from a noun to a verb." What is so insightful about Brad's guidance is that marketers traditionally considered mobile as a singular screen or channel, all too often confining their strategies and planning to what happens on the mobile device alone. But if we consider that the smartphone goes almost *everywhere* with its owner, from the mall, to the gym, and even into the bathroom, we need to expand our thinking by considering *the world around the individual* as a sequence of opportunities to drive that person to do something with their device. In other words, an integrated marketing strategy that includes mobile is a strategy that can and should incorporate the *offline* world as much as it does the *online* world.

With mobile marketing and mobile commerce, there is an incredible imperative to go through what some agencies would label a day in the life exercise. Following target consumers to observe what their typical day looks like—from bed to work, back to bed and all the moments in between—provides a brand or agency with key insights into the behaviors and routines that define a flow of marketing opportunities. What this means, in an era where more time and effort are put into making sense of big data (the wealth of clickstream data that the Internet is helpfully throwing off), is that the key to an integrated communications strategy that truly incorporates mobile (the verb) needs to look more at *little* data. Qualitative research, such as ethnographic studies that physically shadow target consumers to directly observe their offline behaviors, are crucial to fleshing out the common scenarios, usage patterns, and message exposure of mobile consumers, from the billboards they pass, to the radio station they listen to in the car, to advertising on the carts they shop with, and even in public restrooms.

In every case, the glue that holds together an integrated messaging strategy is mobile—and even communications that might seem analog or not mobile can and should have mobile components, because, as we already established, consumers always have a smartphone at the ready. To make sense of the daily journey of a target audience, then, is more than simply studying its online behavior. Businesses have a growing responsibility to understand where the communications windows and opportunities exist within the day to help customers, both online and offline, and the common denominator for both is the mobile phone.

In other words, a mobile strategy is not just a digital strategy: *All* media is in play with the pervasive and ubiquitous presence of a smartphone. No matter what your marketing specialty may be, whether outdoor media, direct mail, television, radio, or email, you must consider that a mobile phone is nearby at the exact moment that your media is read or seen. So you need to consider not only what you want consumers to read, hear, or see, but also what you want consumers to *do* with that message, given that they have the Internet in their pocket.

Weaving your brand's marketing message and customer utilities into the fabric of life's moments is the great challenge and opportunity of mobility. Publicis Groupe's Rishad Tobaccowala, chair of Digitas LBi and Razorfish, told us in an interview, "mobility...frees us to be where we want to be with whom we want to be. Those are highly analog moments. If you see on social platforms what people are doing, they are talking about friends, food, and places." Community managers who oversee inbound customer posts and comments in social media and blogs see this as a way to leverage storytelling with promotions and other marketing messaging. As Tobaccowala also noted, "brands and people are moved by stories, and stories by themselves are not the zeros and ones that drive so much of digital media. Stories are built on maybes, could be's, should have happened, would have happened." Mobility is an incredible facilitator for these stories, because smartphones enable humans to tell the stories of their experiences wherever and whenever they are having them—and in the manner that is most comfortable to them, even if it's a quick photo of dinner or a video of somebody bowling. Any storyteller knows that setting—the place of a story—is every bit as important as the characters. Mobile technology weaves the importance of place into the stories that humans tell each other, and into the stories that brands can tell and co-create with those people.

Capitalizing on the timeliness of activity is one of the several insights that a constant observation of behavior and data can provide to a marketer. If your task is to drive traffic and sales, being present in the appropriate moments through the ideal media experiences is critical, and mobile can help bind together previously unconnected media. This requires us, as Tobaccowala reminds us, to completely rethink what mobile phones are really used for and why. The smartphone especially is more than simply a communications device—it's also used for discovery, entertainment, and as a repository of information and memories. Imagining *all* the ways we can use that kind of device in every conceivable setting for communications requires marketers, advertisers, and communicators to adopt a far more complex model for how, when, where, what, and why they communicate.

To think of the mobile ecosystem as only technology and digital media that happens or is used on that device limits the opportunities to connect with existing and prospective customers. And when you consider where mobile phones are used, it's clear that confining your efforts to online marketing and dismissing traditional, analog, or offline media is a sure way to see your mobile marketing efforts fail. In Figure 9.1, you can see a combination of digital, on-device capabilities and other media that can play a role for creating mobile engagement and actions at the right time and in the right place—and the center for those interactions (indeed, the only glue that likely ties all these interactions together) is the mobile phone.

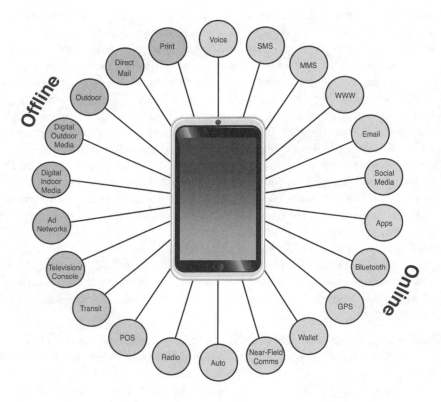

Figure 9.1   *The mobile ecosystem of functions, media, and capabilities.*

What's Old Is New

It is no surprise that so many of the newsmakers in mobility are technologists, developers, and venture capitalists funding startups that have engineered mobile apps to find the best meal or a live music show near you. In Chapters 10–18, we look further into device-specific technology and how to successfully apply several current and emerging mobile assets and tactics to marketing and business. The critical thing for marketers to understand before they get into the technological considerations for their audience, however, is to also think through existing media, places, and channels where and when customers may be driven to purchase.

In that sense, a mobile strategist has to be more of a behavioral strategist—or generalist—than a technologist. Whenever Tim is approached at conferences to explain mobile strategy, for instance, he often starts with email or even outdoor campaign ideas as the first step or phase of a mobile marketing effort. He follows up with a series of simple questions: "Do you or someone else in your organization manage your social media efforts?" "How often does that person sit down for coffee with the direct mail team? The events team? The earned media or corporate communications team?" The message here is clear—if you are going to have an integrated mobile marketing campaign, you need to facilitate internal integration and collaboration among any number of line and staff employees that may have traditionally had very little interaction or even been compartmentalized into silos. But the center of any mobile-enabled marketing effort can never be any one department in an organization—the center has to be the consumer: what they are doing and where, and how they can interact with your brand to tell stories and take meaningful actions.

In discussing certain challenges to traditional business models created by widespread smartphone use, Jennifer Polk, research director at Gartner, explains, "There has been a fundamental shift in customer behavior brought about by advancements in mobile technology, specifically smartphones, which have created an expectation of a channel-agnostic customer experience. This expectation applies to B2B and B2C, and extends across nearly every industry, from media to retail."[1] In another Gartner report, Polk lays out the threat of existing friction between marketing functions and departments, "Creation of channel-agnostic customer experiences will require a joining of forces from all marketing and communication factions. Of course, competition between teams within companies and between external service providers stands in the way, but the success of sales and marketing to a digital consumer hangs in the balance. Internal teams will have to think beyond their roles and break out of organizational silos. Service providers will be forced to come to grips with their real competencies versus their competitive aspirations. Success will depend on collaboration more than competitive forces."[2]

These types of collaborations and the integrated strategies born from them will dictate whether agencies and brands are able to wrap their heads around the offline

---

1. "How Digital Marketers Can Find Hidden Opportunities in Showrooming Risks," Gartner, August 21, 2013.
2. "Blurred Lines: How Digital Marketing Has Created the Ultimate Mashup," Gartner, August 27, 2013.

and physical user experience and how that is tied into digital experiences and purchase behavior. Looking at how digital media can lead to offline experiences also is increasingly necessary for some retail and other brick-and-mortar businesses.

In the Google/Nielsen Life360 Mobile Search Moments Q4 2012 study,[3] it was found that 77% of mobile searches occur at home or at work, while 17% of mobile searches are happening "on-the-go," and that 55% of these searches result in conversions (defined as store visits, a phone call, or purchase) that happen within one hour following the mobile search. Eighty-one percent of conversions triggered by mobile search occur within 5 hours. Further, the study found that 45% of all mobile searches are goal-oriented and conducted to make a decision. In other words, when people go to their mobile phones at the dinner table, while on the couch, or while sitting in a boring office meeting they are looking for answers or to make a decision—there is *intent*. Perhaps they saw something on television or recalled a message heard or seen during the morning commute that served as a reminder to inquire about a product or specific purchase. In other words, they are precursors to an action or a decision.

Marketers can get a step ahead of the prospective customer (or at least meet them where they are) by ensuring that all media and communication have simple and logical calls to action that drive traffic to both digital and physical points-of-purchase. Consider the audience *line of sight*, which may include a billboard, cocktail napkin, newspaper ad, or signage in mass transit stations and train stops. Visual queues and persuasive messaging that are followed by a request to visit a website or to send a text message for more information may be the gateway to incremental sales for many businesses. A business that makes mobile a central part of its marketing and operations strategy stands to gain competitive advantages and benefit from the opportunity to engage the growing population of an always-connected consumer.

Creating and planning cross-media strategies include television and other personal computing devices, as well. Rishad Tobaccowala states, "These devices interact with other devices. Many people have done research that shows there is a cross-screen behavior where you may start in one place and you end up in another place across devices. But, the other behavior we are seeing a lot of is a two-screen simultaneous behavior. Almost everyone is now used to two screens: a tethered screen (like a television) and a screen that they hold in their hand, which increasingly is either a phone or a tablet. We are seeing that when there's content on television, they spend most of their time looking at that, and when an ad comes on they spend most of their time looking at the other device. In two-screen behavior, the mobile device is the interactive device." Today, many social networks, agencies, and

---

[3.] http://think.withgoogle.com/databoard/media/pdfs/creating-moments-that-matter_research-studies.pdf

marketing software firms are trying to build a manageable analytics and content delivery bridge between television and smartphone use.

Mobile Integration in Action

As discussed in this chapter, mobility lets marketers reimagine and rethink the limits and capabilities of all the channels at their disposal. There's no better example of this than the recent campaign by mentoring organization City Year, an effort that won a Groundswell Award from Forrester in 2013 for using social media to drive measurable, actionable results.

City Year is an organization dedicated to recruiting young adults to serve for one year as a mentor for college-going students in high-poverty areas. Because members of the City Year corps serve as role models and resources to encourage students to stay in school and graduate, identifying high-performing young adults to serve is obviously a high priority for City Year. As their Groundswell Award application states,[4] research indicated that potential corps members trusted their peers far more than they trusted institutions, so they devised a campaign focused on driving social traffic to Twitter using the hashtag #makebetterhappen.

Where mobility comes into play here is in the innovative way they incorporated an *offline* medium into the successful execution of this campaign. As a part of this effort, City Year and its agency, Allen & Gerritsen, placed billboards throughout urban areas and other prime locations to attract high-performing young adults. The billboards featured messaging around City Year's mission and focus, but the intriguing part was that there was no URL, no phone number, nor any other direct contact information on these billboards (see Figure 9.2).

Instead, City Year's offline campaign used a *hashtag*—a small snippet of text that allows users of Twitter (in this instance) to tag and locate content. By using only the hashtag #makebetterhappen, these billboards simultaneously provided socially active users with a means to interact with City Year *and* enabled a rich stream of content from user submissions to the hashtag that did more than simply talk about the success of City Year corps members and mentees, but also *showed* those successes with images and stories that were tagged with the #makebetterhappen hashtag.

Before the ubiquity of smartphones (and in the demographic City Year was trying to recruit, smartphones are indeed ubiquitous), a billboard with no discernable call to action or contact information might have driven awareness but not necessarily participation. Today, however, the hashtag on a billboard is contact information, motivation, and a call to action all rolled up in one. City Year's billboard strategy

---

4. "City Year: #makebetterhappen," 2013 Forrester Groundswell Awards Winners, http://groundswell-discussion.com/groundswell/awards/winners.php?y=2013.

was absolutely a mobile strategy, enabling the right targets for the campaign to respond and interact with City Year and its content immediately in the moment wherever they saw the message.

Figure 9.2 *A billboard demonstrating City Year's use of Twitter in an offline message*

As a result, according to Allen & Gerritsen,[5] City Year saw awareness of the program jump 84%. On college campuses where the City Year messaging was displayed, the number of students who either applied or intended to apply jumped by 500%, and the percentage of students who saw City Year as "an ideal employer" nearly quadrupled. Not bad for some billboards! Of course, there were other online and social media elements to this campaign, but the point here is clear—thanks to the smartphone, *every* moment is potentially a mobile moment.

Big Idea

As you are required to think more about the implications of mobile being the primary device used for communication with customers (through many channels both on the device and beyond it), consider how you will tackle integration of traditional and digital media strategies. You may discover that trailing-edge media channels, such as print, radio, and out of home, may be rich resources to identify

---

5. Forrester Groundswell Awards, Allen & Gerritsen, http://www.a-g.com/award-submissions/ Forrester-Groundswell-Awards.

professionals who truly think mobile and how communications can adopt a local mindset to optimally take advantage of place- and time-defined media. You may also find that veteran corps from traditional media organizations inherently may be some of the most insightful digital folks in the room in terms of their ability to leverage heritage media to drive online actions.

What will happen as mobile commerce is adopted as the new norm for purchases and financial transactions is a distinct change in how marketers plan and execute their media, campaign, and awareness efforts. This requires marketers to rethink *everything* with the mobile consumer at the *center* of all other channels and strategies. Companies that can change their mindset today, put the customer's offline life at the center of their strategies, and foster internal collaboration throughout their organizations stand to realize the greatest opportunities for success in the coming age of mobility.

10

Mobile, Media, and Data—Oh My!

The smartphone allows people to share nearly every aspect of their lives via text messages, email, social platforms, and yes, even phone calls. Whether you are an oversharer or not, it is not difficult to understand that a massive flow of data is coming from these devices, no matter who is using them or what they are sharing. For mobile marketing and mobile commerce to reach their full potential, businesses need to be able to collect, parse, and analyze these new data, and the contexts in which that data is generated. But first, a tangled mess of data and systems must be addressed before we can even begin to tap the potential of mobile data.

In Chapter 9, "Collaboration and Integration Are Critical," we discussed seeing mobile as the glue that holds together the various parts of a marketing campaign—it is the only thing that can truly be said to touch all the media, devices, and touch points to which a consumer may be exposed. Similarly, mobile can provide the glue for all the disparate sources of data that marketers have access to, which is good news for marketers who have been praying for the ability to grasp purchase attribution—what people buy, where and why they buy it, the time of day, even who is the buyer. Mobile makes this all possible.

Attribution, or determining what channel(s) contributed to the eventual purchase of a good or service, is one of the most challenging issues that marketers face when it comes to optimizing their efforts. After all, if you don't have a clear picture of which media or messages had the biggest impact on a conversion or purchase, you cannot allocate resources as efficiently as you otherwise could if you had that information. It is easy to be deceived about attribution in a digital world. For example, every move we make online can be tracked, attached to cookies that can be read by Google Analytics or other web tracking software, and then tied to an online purchase, which might lead us to believe that we know what drove the purchase.

However, digital attribution tracking has a gigantic blind spot—the offline world. Consider this: If you hear about a product from a friend in an offline conversation and then search for information about that product before purchasing it, the search engine you use to obtain that information will likely get the credit for driving you to that purchase. However, it was the untrackable conversation you had with your friend that really played the pivotal role in that conversion—and that conversation is essentially invisible to online analytics packages.

Mobile materially changes the game here, because with a mobile device, offline and online are merged in a way we have never seen before. Imagine a kiosk or other form of messaging inside a shopping mall that advertises a new product and provides a URL for information. In the premobile world, a consumer would have to remember or write down that URL or the name of the product for a later search back home or at the office. Today, however, that ad can come with a call to action that features a specific mobile-friendly URL, hashtag, or QR code that can immediately be accessed by the out-of-home consumer, and that trigger can be tied directly to the offline advertisement.

We are big believers in offline media, as previous chapters have surely made clear, and it is our belief that as mobile begins to remove the friction between awareness and action in the offline world, more robust models for attribution will come forward and allow for more complex and appropriate acknowledgement of the role of things like print, radio, billboards, and other offline advertising and marketing vehicles.

Consider radio, for instance. Media buyers have known for years about the power of radio to deliver advertising messages to consumers on the go and to drive out-of-home actions like sending consumers to local movie theaters, restaurants, car dealers, and other retail businesses. Radio ads always feature specific calls to action, and often those calls to action have associated codes or other unique identifiers that establish radio as the source of the message. But when those calls to action rely on a consumer's remembering something to take an action later, there is naturally going to be some attrition or friction that erodes the maximum potential of that message.

With mobile, however, an instantaneous action can be taken, no matter where or when the message is heard, and a signifier can be associated with that action that makes it clear that the message originated with radio. This not only results in a removal of that barrier between awareness and action, but it also provides better data about the attribution of that action, which makes for smarter marketers.

In fact, many radio stations all across the country now embrace mobile technology and have for several years. Mobile has been a complete game changer for some buyers of radio advertising who are looking for better ROI and more accurate attribution for their advertising efforts.

What is powerful about some of these efforts is that many of them don't even require consumers to have smartphone or download an app. In fact, one of the most powerful tools in the arsenal of radio sales staffs is none other than the humble text message, or SMS.

Because a shortcode (a four- or five-digit number to which text messages can be sent) and message can be uniquely assigned to an offline action, that action can be tracked and directly attributed to a radio campaign in ways previously impossible or at least difficult to show. This results in better data and more accurate ROI inputs for buyers and advertisers, which in turn helps to optimize future marketing expenditures.

One radio executive told us of a promotion that a radio station ran with a local professional sports team to give away some highly sought-after playoff tickets. In the promotion, listeners were asked live on the air to text a word to a radio station-owned shortcode to qualify for the drawing. The result? Tens of thousands of texts in about ten minutes. Now, yes, the call to action here was likely irresistible to local sports fanatics, but isn't it always incumbent upon marketers to generate compelling calls to action? The real point here is that an audio message, likely heard by consumers in places where they did not have ready access to a desktop computer, generated this number of responses in less than a quarter of an hour. Without the mobile component of this campaign, it seems highly unlikely that this kind of immediate, in-the-moment response would be possible. And this promotion is also a great example of the fact that the only limit on capitalizing on mobility is creativity, not technology.

The net result, again, of promotions like this is more than simply a win for radio, it's a win for marketing analysts who need better, more precise attribution metrics for their efforts. Mobile gives marketers the ability to not only generate more data, but more contextually relevant data—and that leads to better decisions.

Brands can capitalize on the big data opportunity made possible by mobile device use in three major ways:

- Improved marketing spend and media performance
- Personalization and contextual content and media experiences
- Improved operational efficiency and reduced costs

For a business to capitalize on these opportunities, executives and marketing leadership must understand the great dichotomy of media fragmentation and media convergence caused by multiple device use and mobile ubiquity. This is different with each brand, product, and audience segment, and those segments will grow in number as adoption and use of mobile computing devices grows.

At the forefront in addressing this challenge is Dallas-based OnPoint Marketing Technologies. Cindy Kenyon, cofounder and CEO of OnPoint, sees enormous opportunities in the ever-fragmenting media landscape for marketers that are able to take advantage of—and measure—the increasingly complex landscape of messages to which consumers are exposed. Kenyon states, "There is a lack of industry standards in attribution models for determining media value by cross-device, cross-channel, cross-medium or by user or market. And, not all measurement tools can give you the full picture. It's easy to over-credit some channels and attribution can get political when multiple agencies are involved." As we have seen in the Entercom example earlier, mobile can help to mitigate that overcrediting, and smart marketers work that ability into every possible campaign or effort, whether or not the campaign is seen as a mobile initiative.

Just as the entire sales funnel is collapsing for most businesses, a company's decreasing ability to see the entire scope of media performance and influence over purchase activity is a formidable challenge. Brands stand to reduce operational expenses and grow and sustain revenue when they successfully leverage data from each medium across the planning and placement of other media efforts, while overlaying the view of how each marketing and media channel affects each other and sales results. If you measure the efficacy of a website, mobile app, and email, you must also weigh the influence that outdoor, radio, and direct mail have in driving sales, as well as the influence each and all of these media have on one another. In addition to monitoring the performance of each channel on a consistent real-time basis, marketers should also begin modeling and forecasting how much—and where and when—to invest to yield certain marketing returns. In a world of increasingly better data, it is the marketers who can truly model the online and offline world in terms of attribution who will develop a lasting strategic advantage.

As many marketers begin to understand that social and mobile media attention requires them to more closely measure and monitor attribution of media (earned and paid) and owned assets (websites, email, apps, customer/loyalty programs), they will be met by a complex ecosystem, and one that can truly be said to require both art and science to analyze. After all, most marketers working with this kind of complexity are required to develop their own algorithms for data to square disparate data sources, and as we like to say, algorithms are "math plus assumptions." In fact, as OnPoint's Kenyon notes, "weighting and metric definitions are highly subjective, the data methodologies and analytics conflict with each other, and insights almost always change over the course of a campaign. What's next for data and media analysis is for brands to merge data silos into a single view then implement applied analytics, define a single comparable metric, and integrate strategic insights across the entire media mix." Complicating this is the shift we see from paid media budgets, which are declining (but relatively straightforward to quantify), to earned and owned media, which are incredibly powerful but more difficult to quantify for media mix modeling.

As smartphones increasingly become the primary device used for search and discovery, data analysis and insights will play a major role in serving content to users that then spurs them to action and purchase. As discussed in Chapter 2, "Mobile Is a Behavior, Not a Technology," mobile device use produces attention and impression challenges to brands caused by content consumption being split between email, browsers, and apps, along with decreasing attention spans and incredible amounts of inbound user-generated data coming from smartphones. All this activity should increase the delivery of experiential, behavioral-based, and rules-driven content that engages a customer in real-time by delivering actionable triggers and incentives that more effectively convert search and discovery into action and purchase.

What's a CMO to Do with All This Data?

It is logical to think that the companies with the largest budgets and more advanced or aggressive marketing departments will be the first to address the media mess described earlier in this chapter. As 2014 sees a majority of the world carrying a mobile phone, with a growing portion of that majority being smartphones, we will begin to see true competitive advantages established by those brands that apply technology and data to business strategy and marketing on a daily, instantaneous basis.

As the volume of media channels and digital touch points continues to grow, data will seemingly come from everywhere. Everyone who sits in the marketing suite will soon be expected to participate or manage data insights and answer questions about the cross-discipline performance of their efforts. Some of the mandates these organizations will face include the following:

- Integrating and blending traditional media with emerging media—
  "Is our outdoor media driving email subscriptions?"

- Accounting for social media activity that results in purchases—
  "How much of our Facebook audience is actually buying?"

- Leveraging cross-platform media planning and buying opportunities—
  "Have we aligned *drive-time* digital transit media with our Internet
  radio spots?"

- Reconciling customer inquiries and search with transactions and supply chain data—"Are we moving more product at certain times of day,
  and do we know who's buying from where?"

- Visualizing their cross-device and cross-channel data in a single view—
  "How is video performing through gaming consoles versus tablets,
  search versus email?"

- Implementing attribution models that account for more comprehensive metrics across multiple devices, channels, touch points—"Let's
  take a look at the most common journeys that our loyalty members
  make to the store or to order online, across our mobile app, in-store
  experiences, direct mail and radio calls to action, and the two ways we
  reached or touched them prior to that."

There are different vantage points and data perspectives that a business can now
leverage to examine audiences to segment and analyze their behaviors. Brands that
truly understand their ideal customers beyond simple demographics and high-level
behavioral traits have an advantage over their competitors. Looking at the individual person—and being able to personalize and be relevant at any given moment—
from any device will soon be standard for marketing because of mobile device use.
Today, marketers are starting to look at many more ways to do this, and this leads
to advances in marketing automation and behavioral segmentation, and to deeper
insights that can drive much more relevant and personalized experiences between
a brand or a business and its customers. To do this, a business also needs to cen-
tralize data from multiple systems, media, and owned communications assets, as
illustrated in Figure 10.1.

The commerce implications around leveraged data and insights can be huge when
a brand starts to see the cross-media view of linkages between a mobile coupon,
a print ad, a newspaper impression, a TV commercial, and other disparate media
channels. Mobile presents the ability to influence *all* of those things as the glue that
connects all of them together and facilitates transactions across the board. With
a centralized and integrated data effort in place, mobile facilitates a much more
instantaneous system for converting sales through any and all media, as illustrated
in Figure 10.2.

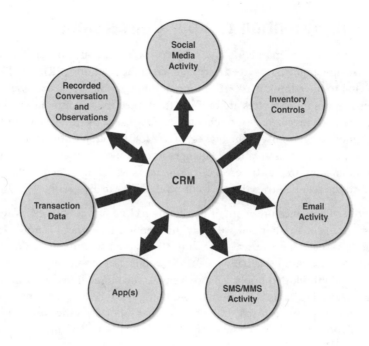

Figure 10.1 *An illustration of a centralized data management system—it is not this easy.*

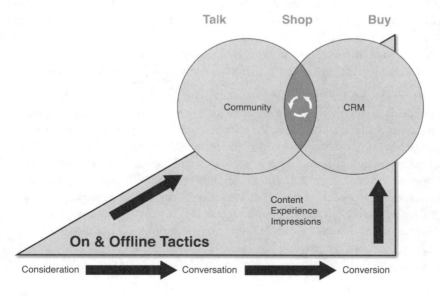

Figure 10.2 *A simplified view of how purchase decisions may be immediately influenced by data-based marketing and media efforts. Credit: Keith Dudley.*

Measuring Attention to Spur Conversions

Of the many facets of marketing and brand communications impacted by mobile device use, none may be as greatly affected as public relations (PR). The PR function is vital to the adoption and education of many mobile apps and assets. As new apps and mobile services are brought to market, most companies will be attempting to change behavior to encourage their usage by mobile consumers. As well, mobile device use is the biggest driver for adoption of the Internet and social media, and this is creating challenges in the way information and images are shared on location in real-time. Smartphone users with HD cameras will forever be the first to the scene of tragedy, crisis, or other newsworthy events.

Christopher Penn, vice president of marketing technology at Shift Communications, told us in an interview, "PR has changed in that a brand is now expected to respond to its customers in real-time...and clients are beginning to realize that the *public* in public relations actually means the public, not media relations. Too many executives still think that public relations equals media relations when in reality it actually means 'Hey, this is the public, and that guy in the Starbucks next to you tweeting on his phone is just as important as that reporter in the *New York Times* because if you screw up, you'll be lambasted in a way that can only be described as spectacular.'"

For Penn and other savvy PR executives, mobile provides a much more direct linkage between awareness and action, and this has an enormous impact on the role of public relations in business and how the silos between PR and marketing and other functions have to break down. As Penn tells it, "If PR's job is to get people lining up at the front door and the front door is locked, then you're going to lose money no matter what. If you're not configured to handle the new technologies, then all the PR in the world is not going to help you, and you will go out of business."

All this means that the PR industry now has to grapple with the complexities of mobile data and fragmented media like never before (which is, of course, an opportunity for forward-thinking PR agencies and others who meet these complexities head on). Mobile's disruption of media is driving PR executives, marketing executives, and sales and support staff all to embrace metrics, understand how to measure the benefits of their efforts, and most importantly put the mobile consumer at the center of their efforts. As Penn says, "The idea of a *mobile first* world is still foreign to a lot of folks, and the bigger the company gets, the less adoption of that viewpoint there is," which might seem counterintuitive but the larger the company, the more systems and processes it has in place that are based on a desktop paradigm.

Dual Screening

It is also important to note that the widespread adoption of smartphones and tablets has a profound effect on how television programs and other media are consumed—which adds further complexity to the kinds of data we have to parse. Often called *dual screening* or second-screen use, the simultaneous use of a tablet or mobile phone while watching television is where compelling calls to action in advertising and product placements can drive purchase behavior from anywhere that broadcast media is viewed or seen. From the couch, the sports bar, in bed, and at the dinner table, smartphone and tablet users are empowered to immediately research brands and products to which they are exposed. Indeed, as a recent study from Nielsen revealed, 72% of smartphone shoppers who make a purchase with their device do so in their homes[1]—and if those purchases are spurred by watching a television program in the offline world, the linkage between message and action is again a potential complication for attribution measurement. Consider that a mobile phone user sitting on the couch might see an ad and then search for the product advertised with an online search engine. A strictly digital measure would give the search engine the credit for driving the online action, but really it served as little more than a utility to connect the user with a product that they were already interested in, thanks to the offline television ad. In addition, those users who are also active with social media such as Twitter and Facebook are also prone to interact with other program fans in those networks during commercial breaks, where even more messages and word-of-mouth marketing can have an effect on a second-screen purchase.

This convergence of media consumption and digital activity is changing the way media is planned and placed by advertisers. Integrated marketing programs that account for multiscreen use in media planning are beginning to reflect this. Multiscreen media planning and management are now complicated by issues such as duplicated reach. For example, if a consumer watches TV and uses her mobile phone and tablet to browse the Web simultaneously, time spent on those devices is a net addition to her TV viewership. What value does the advertiser place on the net addition? Does it get the same weight as TV viewership? Less because television engaged the consumer in the first place, or more value because mobile and tablets are interactive, thus engagement occurs over a longer period of time? Or, should TV's weight be downgraded since the viewer's attention is divided? Or, is it all increased if the second-screen content is designed to be viewed in conjunction with

---

1. "A Mobile Shopper's Journey: From the Couch to the Store (And Back Again)," Nielsen, August 12, 2013, http://www.nielsen.com/us/en/newswire/2013/a-mobile-shoppers-journey--from-the-couch-to-the-store--and-back.html.

the TV programming, such as social TV and second screen apps? Multiscreen campaign management, measurement, fragmentation, and a lack of standards are well-documented issues facing marketers who want to capitalize on this convergence.

Responsible Use of Data

Mobile presents a wealth of insights for companies to improve their business processes, accelerate new product innovation, improve customer service, drive lead generation, cross-sell and up-sell performances, heighten brand awareness, and more. The reality is that data from these devices stands to improve business performance while making customers happier. Marketers will get smarter and use data to their advantage, and this will only be successful over time if there is the responsible, plausible, and reasonable application of data and marketing. That is the big data conundrum right now—you can have all the data in the world, but if you cannot tell stories from it and derive insights from it, it can be useless.

Finally, there is the issue of data privacy and security. OnPoint's Kenyon states, "Consumers complain—and legitimately so in many cases—about data privacy, but at the same time they expect very exacting and highly personalized experiences." This dichotomy between *know me and show me you know me* and *leave me alone* only compounds the challenges of planning for marketing and a brand's responsible use of customer data. Clearly, this is no easy solution, and the future success of big data efforts entails finding the appropriate balance between customer privacy and business innovation. Enterprises have to develop policies that balance their intent and interests from collected data while at the same time serving consumers who want to protect their privacy and security.

A responsible use of data is going to deliver a better life to both businesses and consumers. So how do businesses ensure this responsibility? The answer is simple—and yet not. Above all, your customer must be at the center of all media planning and placement, instead of the medium, channel, or device being used. Putting the person first is surely the ticket to a responsible use of data; happy, well-served customers; and a value exchange on both sides.

11

Visual Storytelling

"Who needs words anymore? Humans have always been visual storytellers. Today, the technology in your pocket makes it easier than ever to take great photos and tell visual stories."

—Jamie Thompson, CEO, Pongr

It is often said that a picture is worth a thousand words. That is especially true for smartphone users who use photos to share opinions, memories, and other experiences with friends, family, and social network connections. As more people walk around with a camera on their mobile phone that is as powerful as most standalone digital cameras, they are sharing as much visual content as text content in social media. To Facebook alone, an average 350,000,000 photos are uploaded daily. But this activity isn't confined to social media: Many of the photos being shared are sent directly to another person via text messaging and email, which presents a challenge to companies that want to understand visual content being shared online by customers as those photos are not public. Still, there are many ways that business-generated and user-generated images may help drive traffic and sales through visual storytelling.

Social media started out as a progression of chat tools that allowed people to conduct a conversation through text in real-time via a connected computer. We use the term "connected computer" instead of simply "the Internet," as we can recall the days of having a CompuServe account during the 1980s in which we could argue four-stroke motorcycle engine superiority over two-stroke engines with people all over the United States inside a chat room. This basic ability to host text-driven conversations through a computer stayed literally grounded with desktop computers and notebook computers that required a wired Ethernet connection until the arrival of the camera phone in the late 1990s. Even after Wi-Fi connectivity became a popular amenity in a few coffee shops within major urban areas, you didn't exactly walk into a place and see people taking photos with the cameras built in to their notebook computers.

As Internet service providers (ISPs) began to increase bandwidth to improve connection speeds and certain entrepreneurs began to see the opportunity to digitize photo albums, things began to change. Photo-sharing websites gained in popularity in the late 1990s and early 2000s as computer USB ports empowered mobile peripherals such as digital cameras and cell phones to be connected and download captured images. In June 1997, Phillippe Kahn became the first person documented to send photos from a cell phone, instantly sharing images of his newborn daughter, Sophie, with more than 2,000 people around the world.[1] From that moment, the race was on to bring the camera phone to market.

Today, with smartphones being a constant companion in our daily lives, our ability and desire to document and share experiences as they happen serves our need to ask for help, archive memories, and to tell stories. The photo album that used to sit on the coffee table for visitors to browse has become a digital album available through social networks and mobile photo-sharing applications. When shopping or considering a purchase of any size, it is easy for someone to capture a photo and immediately send it to a friend to get their opinion or guidance. This reality means that companies have as much to learn from the photos and images that their customers share as they do from managing a consistent program of visual storytelling that drives conversion to online and offline points of business and purchase.

While this behavior brings new challenges to companies who listen to social conversations (more on that in a later chapter), it also gives great opportunities to brands for discovering and building meaningful relationships with brand advocates as part of their digital and social marketing efforts. A prime example

---

1. Wikipedia, http://en.wikipedia.org/wiki/Phillipe_Kahn

of branded visual storytelling is NASA. When it comes to driving awareness and education through engaging content, there are probably few brands beyond entertainment that can make all of that happen and ignite brand advocates as fast as NASA can. "We're constantly looking to expand our social media portfolio to include tools that will best tell NASA's story of exploration and discovery," said NASA Press Secretary Lauren Worley. "Instagram has a passionate following of users who are hungry for new and exciting photos. We believe we have some of the most engaging images on and off the planet—and we can't wait to engage with Instagrammers."[2]

A little more than 24 hours after NASA launched its organizational Instagram account on September 6, 2013, it had more than 44,000 followers (see Figure 11.1) with only one rocket launch (see Figure 11.2) and just seven photos posted. Talk about lift-off!

Figure 11.1 *The NASA Instagram account profile, showing 44,000 followers, a little more than a day after the account was opened.*

2. "NASA to Share the Universe with Instagram Users through Its Images," NASA press release, September 6, 2013, http://www.nasa.gov/press/2013/september/nasa-to-share-the-universe-with-instagram-users-through-its-images.

Figure 11.2 *As NASA prepared for the launch of its LADEE spacecraft, photos of the moon and the launchpad were shared through Instagram.*

Leveraging User-Generated Photography

"Now, consumers are using photography daily to drive a massive amount of conversation everywhere they go from a local park to the grocery store checkout line to happy hour with friends," states Brian Zuercher, CEO of Seen. While talking with business owners intrigued by customer-generated photos posted and shared online, Zuercher saw an opportunity for the business to leverage such content. Seen was soon born to help monitor these photos and create campaigns within Instagram and Twitter. Since September 2012, Seen has empowered brands such as the Indianapolis 500, Dodge Ram, and David's Bridal to build customer relationships by automating comments on photos posted using branded hashtags while collecting contact information and insights for follow-up communications.

"We're helping these brands connect with their most passionate and loyal customers through visual marketing," says Zuercher. "Thanks to the influx of visuals being shared across social channels, social listening isn't just about reading what people are saying online—it's also seeing what they're sharing. Photos are rich with context—providing a snapshot into a consumer's life. They're a powerful and informative representation of a consumer's journey and experience with a brand. When someone shares a photo in social media, it provides a glimpse into how that person wants to represent themselves to friends and followers. Brands are able to uncover valuable, meaningful insights only found via visual media."

Public relations and marketing are also critical ingredients for successfully activating a social photo campaign. How well the campaign is activated by integrating several communications efforts together directly correlates to the overall photo campaign's success. "Our clients' campaigns have proven to be an effective way for them to learn more about their customers and build a deeper relationship with them, which in turn leads to sales opportunities" Zuercher says. "Bath & Body Works invited customers to share a photo on Instagram with the hashtag #BBWSweetheart of their favorite 'Sweetheart' product for a chance to win iPad cases and Bath & Body Works prizes. Bath & Body Works aggregated the data from the social photo campaign and compared the social sharing statistics of each product with the POS (point of sale) data to get a comprehensive view of their most social products."

Aaron Strout, from digital agency W2O, has another way of explaining the importance of visual storytelling in social media. In an interview with Strout, he noted "It will be worth paying attention to the impact that mobile photo sharing has on the traditional and widely held 90-9-1 principle—the thesis that 90% of Internet users lurk or read content without interacting, 9% comment or contribute to conversations, and 1% are the real content creators." If a business posts images that are compelling with clear and concise calls to action in social networks, the practice may an incredibly effective way to draw traffic from social media to a point of purchase.

Lisa Joy Rosner is the CMO of Neustar, a real-time information services and analytics company, and former head of marketing for social media analysis company Netbase. Lisa pointed out the importance of visual storytelling in an interview with us, stating that, "Visual storytelling certainly has a big influence on how information spreads. In a study that [Netbase] conducted in partnership with Edison Research, we saw that images pinned to Pinterest are playing a relatively influential role in inspiring women's fashion decisions, when compared to the percentage of women who actually have Pinterest accounts. Brands need to pay attention to those visual channels in social media."

Visual Listening

The non-textual photo and image updates from mobile devices have disrupted many brands' ability to understand sentiment, preferences, and opinions. "We now live in a world where people express themselves visually on Facebook, Twitter, Instagram, Tumblr, Flickr, YouTube, even Foursquare. There's a long tail of sites that are significant places where consumers share visual information. It's easy and fast for anyone to take a good picture and post it into their social network. We made a bet back in 2008 that as the quality of cameras went up, price points went down, and smartphones became the primary Internet device for hundreds of millions of people, pictures would be at the core of how people communicate. Just look at Snapchat. It's a visual communication platform. Who needs words anymore? Humans have always been visual storytellers. Today, the technology in your pocket makes it easier than ever to take great photos and tell visual stories. It has been hugely disruptive," says Jamie Thompson, chief executive of Pongr, in an interview with the authors.

Pongr was founded in 2008 by Thompson and Zach Cox, who serves as chief software architect, after the two worked together at a Cambridge, Massachusetts-based military research and development company, Charles River Analytics. In their quest to build mobile photo applications that would use image recognition to identify products and give consumers purchasing information, they left their jobs and got to work. "After building some of the core visual recognition technology on top of Amazon Web Services, we started getting pulled into advertising campaigns where brands, agencies, and publishers wanted us to help them make their traditional ads into image recognizable direct-response triggers. Thus, we started to build direct mobile marketing tools and capabilities onto the core image recognition service. That led to more mobile marketing via photo-taking and we extended the Pongr platform further to start taking into account loyalty, social sharing, and flexible, fast direct mobile response capabilities," says Thompson.

Curating photos and video that people have been asked to share, or are already publicly sharing in social media, is one way to leverage rich media generated by customers. A unique opportunity with smartphones and tablets is to directly ask (via email, SMS, and other media) customers and prospective customers to upload and share an image through the mobile browser. Such direct communications between a brand and its customer audience can yield powerful results for increased site traffic and provide the brand with intelligence (location, preferences, and opinion, among other insights). Thompson and Pongr have collected a number of fascinating case studies about the intersection of visual storytelling and mobile marketing. To provide a better sense of where these trends are going, here are three, involving Arby's, UNREAL Candy, and Edel Golf.

Case Study: Arby's, Snap and Rock

Through television, in-store signage, and digital media, fast food chain Arby's invited customers to take a photo of their favorite music artist featured on Arby's fountain drink cups, and then email or text it to arbys@pongr.com for a chance to win VIP concert tickets, meals, music downloads, posters, and more. Over eight weeks, more than 660,000 photos were submitted and shared in social media to a total potential audience reached of more than 10.8 million people. Digital banner campaigns that ran alongside the promotion realized a 2.01% click-through rate, representing 20 times more than the average banner campaign and 40 times above the average Facebook campaign. Example assets from this campaign are shown in Figure 11.3.

Figure 11.3 *Examples of campaign assets and user-generated images shared in Arby's Snap and Rock campaign with Pongr.*

Case Study: UNREAL Candy, Unjunked Sweetstakes

Consumers were invited through UNREAL Candy's social network profiles and brand bloggers to take a photo of their UNREAL candy and email or text that image to unreal@pongr.com for a chance to win $10,000 to spend at Target. New customers and existing UNREAL fans drove participation across social media networks with some impressive success beyond industry averages. For instance, 31% of the 1,350 photos that were submitted over a three-week period were also shared on Facebook and Twitter, for a potential total audience reach of more than 306,000. The campaign's click-through rate of 5.43% was substantially better than their average for web banner campaigns and average for Facebook banner performance. Example assets from this campaign are shown in Figure 11.4.

Figure 11.4 *Examples of campaign assets and user-generated images shared in UNREAL Candy's Unjunked Sweetstakes campaign with Pongr.*

Case Study: Edel Golf

Edel Golf is a luxury, customized golf club manufacturer that sells putters, irons, and wedges that usually cost more than $500 each. Through certified fitters—namely through its partnership with Golf Galaxy—Edel customizes each club for a golfer. This makes the company's products highly personalized with high performance expectations. Edel partnered with Together, a marketing campaign platform that delivers app-like experiences through the browser (no download required), to help Edel activate its existing customers, capture rich media, and drive advocacy marketing. Edel had done very little marketing in the past, but it does have a loyal, cultlike following. Edel's clubs are like works of art. Capturing a photo at the height of excitement (when the box is opened), and asking the owner about his success story after 30 days of use provides Edel with ongoing content to fuel its marketing campaigns, as shown in Figures 11.5 and 11.6.

Figure 11.5   *Email sent to all past purchasers of Edel Golf products.*

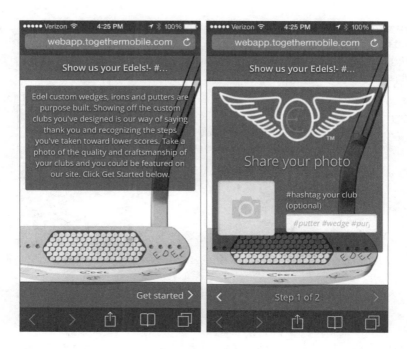

Figure 11.6   *Landing page into the Together web application Edel Golf activation (Get Started) on left, and photo submission page (Step 1) on right.*

The email sent to solicit photos from past Edel purchasers had no incentive or promotional message. Of the people who clicked on the email, 24% submitted a photo (for a 24% response rate) through the browser. The responses primarily came from mobile devices. This represented a personal best for email campaigns for Edel Golf and outperformed industry averages, as shown in Figure 11.7.

Edel's Personal Best – Fantastic email open and click-through rate				
	Photo Collection Campaign*	Edel's List Average	Industry Average (MailChimp)	Industry Benchmark (Epsilon**)
Open Rate	60.5%	53.2%	21.2%	31.3%
Click-Through Rate	8.6%	7.2%	2.8%	5.1%

* Delivered to 3,219 on March 2, 2014 at 12:24 pm CT
** http://www.epsilon.com/pr/Q212emailbenchmarks

Figure 11.7   *Edel Golf photo-sharing email performance.*

Through clearly stated terms and conditions, Edel Golf now has unlimited usage rights for the images submitted through the campaign, and the company also leverages Together's photo wall system to display certain images on the Edel Golf website, as shown in Figure 11.8.

Figure 11.8   *Using the Together photo wall display system, customer-generated photos are displayed on the Edel Golf website and then used across other marketing communications assets and media.*

Capitalizing on Line-of-Sight

Consumers love to be visually stimulated, and as more and more of those visuals are being captured on mobile phones, a big part of a mobile strategy is to ensure that vehicles such as outdoor media, promotional products, business interiors, and even sponsorship messaging at live events are well-designed and visually compelling. Those that are have the possibility to be shared beyond simply the live audience of an event or the original viewer of the promotion or vehicle—thanks to mobile social media, they can be shared everywhere.

What this means is that businesses that have signage, outdoor, or transit media buys as part of their marketing mix should be sure to spell out their Facebook URL or accompany their messaging with a hashtag to draw followers and likes to their social media profiles. Signage, other out-of-home media, and promotional wares, such as drink coasters, table tent signage, and napkins, all present items on which to place a call-to-action message and a URL that leads to a responsive website, which is discussed in Chapter 16, "The Mobile Web."

Also, for brands that invest in experiential marketing programs, trade shows, tours, and event promotions, it isn't enough to simply produce a quality event. To fully capitalize on events and out-of-home experiences, brands should do everything possible to have attendees or participants capture and share photos in social media.

The "Selfie"

If you have the Facebook or Instagram apps on your phone, take a quick look at one of those newsfeeds. Do you see photos of a friend who's smiling ear-to-ear standing on the beach, at a concert, or in the middle of IKEA...by herself? Few things may make smartphone users happier than capturing a self-portrait, or "selfie." Usually they are used to brag, gloat, or show off to friends and family. This is where large logos, outlandish and elegant murals, posters, billboards, and interior designs may compel consumers to snap mobile photographs and share those moments with their friends and family through social media, email, or texting.

For a service business in the home improvement industry—such as painting and landscaping—there are simple ways to generate referral business from current clients: Once a particular job is completed, ask your client if he would like to have a photo of the finished project. Then ask if you can use the client's phone to take the photo. Take a photo of your client standing next to the work (an "assisted selfie," as it were), and then simply hand the phone back to the client. No need to tell him what to do with the photo, as odds are that he will either send it as an MMS text message to family or friends, or share it on a social network. No matter how the client shares the photo, there is always a probability that someone will respond or comment with the question, "Who did the work for you?"

The automotive dealer, repair, or body shop, can do something similar to the preceding example for a service business: Ask a customer if she wants a photo taken with her new or repaired vehicle. Few moments of elation compare to the instant a new set of keys are in one's hand accompanied with a new car smile. The customer can take a selfie next to the car, or the dealer can snap a photo of the customer standing next to her vehicle, and then hand the phone back to her. Who knows? Perhaps in hours or days, a friend of the smiling subject may show up on the lot!

Managing a Visual Storytelling Program

There is no one-size-fits-all direction that a brand can learn or an agency can prescribe on how to use images and photography to engage customers in digital media. Like everything in mobile marketing, each company has unique audiences and special dispositions of customer propensity to respond to what is published and posted online. That being known, here is an informal checklist to help manage visual storytelling in social media that is shared widely and may potentially draw traffic in your direction:

- Use a late model smartphone to capture images. This helps to ensure you take high-quality photos and empowers an instant upload or ability to quickly send to your graphic designer, and to upload directly to a social media profile, photo stream, or online album.

- Respect the data plan. Use high-quality, not high-resolution, images. The higher the resolution is, the larger the file size will probably be, and that may stop users from viewing or downloading the image on their phone due to data charges and slow connection speeds. Use video sparingly for the same reasons.

- Ensure you right-size images for each social media network where they are posted. As dimensions and specifications vary per each network, changing often and sometimes monthly, you want to be sure that you aren't requiring viewers to scroll, zoom, or pinch their screens to see an image in its entirety.

- Incorporate text that spells out a specific call-to-action such as a daily deal or other promotional offer. The narrative of certain company facts and stories and support for causes and community events can drive viewers to share your image with friends or join in your philanthropic efforts. I did this with a photo I shared on Facebook and Twitter to ask friends to contribute to a fundraiser—see Figure 11.9. (Tip: Use a mobile app such as Over—www.madewithover.com—to overlay text on photos from your phone.)

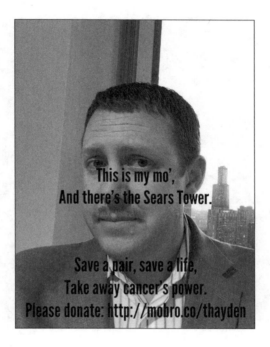

Figure 11.9   *A selfie Tim captured and edited with his smartphone and then shared across Facebook and Twitter to raise funds and awareness for Movember to battle certain types of men's cancer.*

- Be prepared to pay for views. Most social media networks are now requiring businesses to pay to promote their posts, especially those that consist of text and images. This is a trend we should all expect to continue as audiences segment their time spent on certain apps and social media networks and businesses look for new ways to monetize their services through advertising programs.

Finally, it's worth remembering the context of mobile use and the environments in which mobile content is consumed. Mobility means that we have less time and ability to consume and/or respond to the many text messages and emails that are put before us every hour. A compelling visual, however, is instantly arresting in whatever time and place it is consumed. For brands that want to create a lasting impression in the mobile moment, there is no better imperative than to convince consumers to, as the old saying goes, "take a picture—it'll last longer."

12

Mobile Listening and Response

It is entertaining to hear debates between marketers on which channel or media is better to use to reach and convert an ideal audience. Some want to argue social against mobile and vice versa. Tim has often been called upon to defend a stance that someone other than he has made in such debates. One of Tim's former colleagues would tell him, "You don't need to worry about Facebook and Instagram. Those are social media concerns, not mobile." Such conflicts and dismissals may be justified in some minds, yet it is wrong to separate the two. Like peanut butter and chocolate (or jelly for some people), social and mobile live in harmony. In fact, mobile is redefining the future of social media on a daily basis.

As comScore reported in its 2014 *U.S. Mobile App Report*, social media juggernaut Facebook is the most popular mobile app, both in terms of its audience size and the time spent on the app among all the different demographic segments ranging from 18 to 55+.[1] Some First Quarter 2014 Operational Highlights from Facebook's Q1 2014 Earnings Report show how mobile-intensive the world's largest social network is:

- Daily active users (DAUs) were 802 million on average for Q1 2014, an increase of 21% year-over-year.
- Mobile DAUs were 609 million on average for Q1 2014, an increase of 43% year-over-year.
- Monthly active users (MAUs) were 1.28 billion as of March 31, 2014, an increase of 15% year-over-year.
- Mobile MAUs were 1.01 billion as of March 31, 2014, an increase of 34% year-over-year.[2]

Calculated as percentages, 79% of monthly active users and 76% of daily active users are accessing Facebook from a mobile device.

Desktop Blindness

Yet even when research proves that social media is predominately accessed from a mobile device, many marketers find it hard to believe. There are logical reasons why many social media marketers and community managers struggle to understand such use. This is something that Tim calls "desktop blindness": If you sit at a desk and stare at a computer monitor for six-plus hours each day, you are bound to be somewhat ignorant as to what is happening outside that environment, where an always present smartphone is the primary (or sometimes only) screen for social media use. As already discussed in Chapter 2, "Mobile Is a Behavior, Not a Technology," the smartphone fits nicely in a pocket or purse and travels almost everywhere with its owner. Also, during work hours many people can only check Facebook, Twitter, and their favorite blogs via smartphone. This is because many employers today either firewall social media and certain websites or have in place policies that prohibit employees from using social media applications and sites on company-issued devices.

The larger reality here is that the smartphone is an extremely social device. Accompanying its owner on a walk across town, on the commute, at lunch and

1. http://www.comscore.com/Insights/Presentations-and-Whitepapers/2014/The-US-Mobile-App-Report

2. http://investor.fb.com/releasedetail.cfm?ReleaseID=842071

dinner, and at all points in between, the smartphone is a guest at the all-day/all-night party that is life. It is also an instant and personal hotline to share experiences and communicate with friends and family at any given moment. Having social media access on this device creates the ability for offline conversations and online content to be interwoven in real time, a luxurious fact of life for the user who also creates both challenges and opportunities to marketers.

Mobile Is a Busy Place

To frame the challenges and opportunities associated with social marketing today, it is critical to understand that the mobile audience has a number of additional utilities and media on a smartphone and tablet that were not previously available on a desktop or notebook computer. No one truly knows what the cadence or common use patterns and routines for all these newfound activities on a smartphone will be, but they will likely be unique to each user, almost like a digital DNA sequence. If you consider for a moment how your iTunes playlist is all yours and unique, you can see how all of the apps and functions on a smartphone create very unique and personal usage patterns. More than anything, read any statistical or research report that claims to know the *optimal* time for posting to certain social networks, sending email, or placing a location-based banner ad. Any rhythm that exists today is sure to erode in the coming years.

For the social marketer, the complexity of these usage patterns creates a challenge because brands are competing with media, entertainment, and friends and family, all on one tiny screen. Not only is the mobile screen smaller than any desktop computer, but the volume of noise and activity that takes place on the device is already drawing attention away from sustained viewing or perusal of social networks and newsfeeds. This does not mean that smartphone users check their social media accounts less. It merely means that attention to social media streams can be interrupted more often than when viewing happens on a multitabbed browser and column-organized social profile management dashboard such as Hootsuite or TweetDeck.

We learned from talking to many brands and agencies that many desktop behaviors such as email and browser use are still being proven as popular and successful places to capture consumer attention, as tracked with analytics and measurement tools. In Figure 12.1, you can see a displacement of device use activity, desktop versus mobile, illustrating how busy a place a smartphone can be.

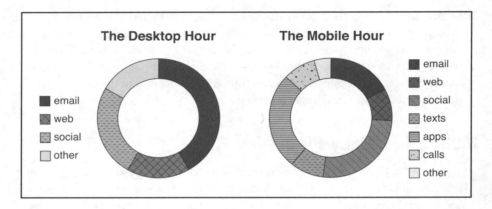

Figure 12.1 *An illustrated comparison of digital functionality and activities, desktop computing versus mobile computing.*

The "Listening" Challenge

The practice of *listening* to social media is one of the most popular ways that a company may identify customer concerns, understand negative and positive mentions of a brand by name, and detect when someone is considering a purchase. Many larger organizations go further with social media monitoring to understand individual preferences and routines and the overall state of brand sentiment in online conversations. Several emerging trends can be attributed to smartphone use that are changing the way social listening may be conducted for brands.

Natural-Language Processing (NLP)

As more people are carrying smartphones with them everywhere they go, many of them are liberated from using uniform *business speak* in their social media conversations. They are likely to use more colloquial language and slang in their posts and brand mentions, perhaps influenced by their culture or region. "The abbreviations, misspellings, and 'slanguage' of the smartphone culture makes it even more important to have smart social listening technology that learns as language changes," states Neustar's Lisa Joy Rosner. These challenges are arriving at the same time that a growing social media audience is posting more content (text, photos, ratings, reviews, and so on) than ever before, making it more difficult for good social intelligence-based business decisions to be made in real-time. Rosner says further that, "The accuracy of data from traditional social listening systems, which utilize basic text analytics that simply look for the mention of specific keywords, are much less accurate in determining the negative or positive sentiment of social posts." Furthermore, recent research[3] performed by research-based consultancy Millward Brown, shows that, in an analysis of more than 30 million conversations, as little as 40% of the total volume of brand conversations may consist of actual mentions of the brand by humans. This shows that auto-response and marketing automation software is posting a majority of many brands' social content, instead of live human responses and posts. When you consider the real-time nature of a mobile-originated social comment or post, an either happy or not-so-happy customer could be standing at the entrance to your business.

Such disparity between *good* and *bad* data affects most of the social media metrics that a company may track and monitor, and it further distorts decisions that marketers may make based on those metrics. NLP technology is critical in boosting both the accuracy of social media data and a brand's ability to intelligently recognize and filter out the junk. This is an especially critical need with enterprise brands that may have a large amount of customers spread across a wide geographic area.

And if it is not slang and natural language that causes an issue, it may well be the shorthand and abbreviated style of updating and posting to social networks that gives marketers a listening headache. "Concise yet complex, mobile updates have abbreviated the average length of a social post while making text analysis much more difficult due to the irregular complexities of processing mobile shorthand. Social listening tools have gotten smarter with natural language processing, machine learning, and complex Boolean 'wildcard' and 'fuzzy' searches. These advances allow the tools to better understand and extract insights from collections of abbreviated, misspelled, and slang terms. Not to mention the fun challenge in deciphering and classifying emoticons, like ;-) and :(," states Adam Beaugh, cofounder of Zignal Labs.

Listening software tools that use NLP are also useful for companies that need to segment social media conversations based on themes or conversation drivers, empowering marketers to find behavioral or psychographic customer segments in addition to traditional demographic (age, gender, ethnicity) groups. Many companies, including Netbase and Zignal Labs, are also delivering new solutions that help large brands identify demographic segments based on social network users' publicly available information. That means that it is now possible to plan and execute actionable marketing based on behavioral information that you simply wouldn't be able to discover through traditional research and many contemporary listening platforms.

---

3. http://www.millwardbrown.com/docs/default-source/insight-documents/articles-and-reports/ Millward-Brown-10-Digital-Prediction-2013-A4.pdf

Real-Time Social Media Management

Many retail, hospitality, and service businesses are also realizing that mobile users often expect an immediate response when they mention a brand in social media, positive or negative. Consider that a restaurant complaint posted on Twitter may be coming from a customer who is sitting at a table just feet away from the manager, and the hotel guest who complains about a lack of hot water may be running late for the conference downstairs. These scenarios of immediacy are not unique to only a few industries, as we've had several social marketers share with us that the past two years have brought dramatic reductions in average response time for customer recovery situations. Even plumbers and home repairmen have told us that they are amazed at how fast a customer can share a photo on Facebook and criticize work they have performed—and how that reduces or increases the following days' call volumes. "What mobile has done to social is made it 100% in the moment, real-time, all the time," says Neustar's Rosner.

Another good example is the wine industry, where multiple stakeholders can benefit from knowing in real-time what people are saying about a specific winery, varietal, or vintage, as well as the time and location of those statements and the wine's consumption. "There is tremendous value in constantly knowing and learning about wine drinkers," says Paul Mabray, CEO and chief strategy officer of Vintank, a social customer relationship management solution for the wine industry. Mabray explains, "Mobile has become the number one outlet for our customers to review and act upon our insights, and it has forced us to focus on providing a mobile app to ensure that Vintank is most effectively used. A social business such as a winery or any business that has employees that are more often remote and removed from a computer than sitting in front of one, especially restaurants, are starting to use a smartphone or tablet in lieu of a computer. To deliver them actionable insights and messages so that they may respond in a timely fashion requires a mobile delivery mechanism."

The urgency for immediate social listening insights and analysis is part of the mobile opportunity for industries including food and beverage, sports and entertainment, software, retail, and many service categories. A company's ability to decipher and react to digital conversations and statements in real-time can determine the success of a sales opportunity, repeat business, and referrals, among a host of other revenue opportunities. For social media monitoring and listening to truly drive sales, intelligence and insights must be actionable for offline commerce situations. Mabray states, "As a former e-commerce guy, I started the company with the basic premise that if we can find people that talk about wine a lot, we can more easily convert that into a tendency to purchase." Known as *Interest Graph Listening*, it was great for Vintank to measure purchase intent, but there were often too many conversations for a winery to sort through and make physically actionable. As such, Vintank has created algorithms to run the conversations through to instantly understand the customer in a contextual capacity. Vintank can quantify a person's purchase intent for a specific wine or winery by using a variation of a simple direct marketing metric, *RFM*, or *recency, frequency, and monetary value*, and coupling that metric with a notion we call *texture*, or all the things said within the conversation and the person's profile.

Vintank also profiles customers much more deeply than around intent alone, whereby the company has integrated Vin65, a SaaS commerce platform owned by WineDirect, with Vintank's social media intelligence tools. Mabray states, "Now millions of transactions are coupled with over 16 million social customers and almost 100 million wine conversations." From this, Vintank can derive more thorough statistics and insights, such as

- How much more does a Facebook or Twitter customer spend than one who is not?
- How much longer is the lifetime value of a social media customer than a non-SM customer?
- Is the average order value of a customer who mentions/interacts with a winery in social media larger?
- Is a lack of social media interaction an early indicator of customer attrition?
- How many interactions in social media result in higher average order values (AOV)?

This is truly groundbreaking, empowering Vintank customers to look at how these observations overlay against *interest graph listening,* proving or disproving that someone who talks about wine actually buys more wine, and other correlations between conversations and commerce. Since most wine and food are talked about through a mobile device in the moment and at the event, mobile is the primary catalyst for them to gain a better understanding of this type of user behavior and determine how to better target and serve customers.

A key in marketing today, period, is to understand who your ideal audience is, the social channels in which they spend the most time, what they are saying online, and where they physically spend money. With that information, social intelligence can help you understand the conversation so you can create and distribute the right content, messaging, and images in the right place at the right time. In 2015 and beyond, mobile usage and advances in data integration will help bring more context to how social media can be leveraged in the shopping experience. This will include localization of content to connect nearby goods and services with buyers and advancements in image recognition where all someone will need to do is point a camera at an object to find where to buy it or from which retailer to order it.

13

Personalization and Relevance

The fields of advertising, marketing, and public relations have always focused on messaging and strategies that audiences would believe were meant for or targeted to them. In media, brand confidence is shaped through imagery, phrases, and emotional scripts as much as product or service quality. Most of what brands and their marketing agencies have done in the past has been to follow what their subjective focus groups and third-party research told them would and would not work for messaging. Alongside that direction, a homogenous audience of consumers would be segmented by demographics such as household income, age, ethnicity, gender, ZIP code, and other details. This method of forming a brand's narrative still works for many companies, and most agencies have started to leverage social media analytics to capture the "voice" and relationship structure between customers to make messaging and media more relevant.

As discussed in Chapter 10, "Mobile, Media, and Data—Oh My!," technologies are available today that allow for media and content to be instantaneously placed and managed to coincide with buying behaviors. There are also many solutions for business that automate certain marketing functions. With the increased use of social media and a changing society with increasingly diverse cultures and ethnic groups, we have seen everything from boutique lifestyle agencies to marketing technology platforms claim that they have the power to find the right audience at the right moment, time, and place. It is true that certain data captured through interactive digital media and customer information can help an agency or brand be more accurate with its messaging content and orchestration of delivering those messages.

However, most of what marketers use as of late 2014 is information limited to that which is purchased from a third party, publicly available on the Internet, or volunteered by a customer. Because so much of this information is caught within a certain time period or frame of mind, can brands consider this a truly legitimate moment of relevancy?

We interviewed Dr. Neal Burns, director of the Center for Brand Research at the University of Texas, who spells out advertising agencies' lack of grasp on context and relevancy thusly: "The advertising business—in the past 10 years from my perspective—failed to recognize the significance of the audience and cultural changes that were taking place. So, except for a few agencies, the business lagged behind. The self-congratulatory nature of creative awards continued to dominate, but the big change was the recognition of the importance of digital messaging and, in particular, mobile social networking. The Internet was, of course, a huge influence on agency strategic considerations, but the demand for attention of that buzz/bell/vibration in our purse or pocket changed the business."

Getting Started

Just as social media and mobile devices sparked new levels of content demand, there are also a number of advantages that these same technologies inherently bring to marketers to meet that demand by delivering more contextual and relevant content. For large and small businesses alike, there are software as a service (SaaS) tools and content management systems that can assist in ensuring that content seen on a mobile-accessed website meets the contextual coordinates of the moment. Coordinates that can help prescribe the best content for the moment come from inbound mobile device and server data that can reveal the device type (phone, brand, operating system, browser, and so on), time (of day, day of the week, and so on), location (by GPS and/or IP address), language spoken, and the terms/words used in a search engine that referred the website visit. This is illustrated in Figure 13.1 as a way to better understand how all these coordinates can work together to deliver a more meaningful experience.

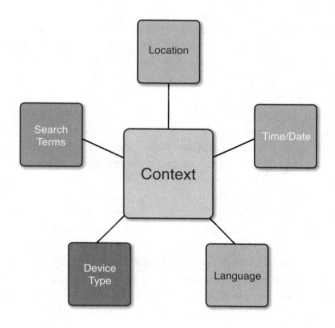

Figure 13.1   *When a mobile user clicks on a website link or enters a URL into a mobile browser, several telling data coordinates may accompany the resulting website hit or visit. Together, these coordinates can help frame a more relevant and contextual content experience for the user.*

Relevance and context are defined in many different ways, and the speed at which new applications and mobile software are coming to market makes it possible to see deeper into the daily routines and life preferences of mobile users. More advanced technologies also can reconcile the social graph of users (their "likes" and "follows," what friends and connections like, where a person spends the most time online) with brand-specific behavior including preferences and opinions shared through polls, surveys, and general mobile app use and e-commerce shopping. Dr. Burns states, "The consumer is a control freak—'don't tell me when and where to shop'; 'I don't care about your hours, I'm online at 2 a.m., and I may decide to shop for shoes or a new suit then'; 'I know how to use the shopping service, and I will buy that camera at the best possible price.'" Burns notes that the ability to know who the customer is (age, education, location, online behavior and sites visited, health, recent travel, purchases, and more) gives the ad agency the ability to deliver personally relevant messages where the content and context have an impact previously unknown.

Even though it has been said that some retailers know that you are pregnant before your mother does based on shopping cart contents and frequency of purchase, the reality of fully knowing your customers takes much more than an impressive arsenal of analytics and customer feedback systems. MyWebGrocer's senior product marketing manager, Rebecca Rouse, works with grocery chains and the brands sold through them, and she tells us that having a constant flow of feedback and customer-volunteered insights is key to converting shoppers. "Location, both situational and contextual, is critical for mobile commerce success," says Rouse. "There is also a big push to create a seamless, personalized experience for shoppers whether they are online via desktop, mobile, or tablet, or in-store on their mobile device. Shoppers are willing to provide information about themselves—email, past purchases, and more—if they receive something valuable in return. Coupons, offers saving them money, or recommendations for quick meals based on items on sale this week, are the best use of personalization and bring value to the shopper, retailer, and brand." David Javitch, vice president of product at ScanBuy sees a similar trend in rewarding customers with deals and discounts for sharing information, as he shared with us in an interview. "It really comes down to relevance and what is right for specific audience segments. The overall trend in mobile will continue to be a move toward conversion and creating loyal customers. This will be driven by mobile couponing solutions that are simpler for both consumers to access and use and brands to distribute and deliver. We believe that brands will also start to use technology to create more relevant experiences in real-time based on individual preferences like location, previous engagement history, company CRM data, and more."

Asking for Directions

Still, businesses and brands must respect that there is no longer a one-size-fits-all approach to content activation and rewarding advocacy, even when there seems to be evidence that audience segments share common preferences, habits, and demographic labels. This is true even when all the inbound data and analytics tell you what a mobile user likes on Facebook and where they are that very second. That's why an effective way to frame the content experience may be to ask a series of questions. A website viewed on a mobile device—a smartphone to be specific—should have fewer overall navigation and content options, and there is the opportunity for a brand to personalize its content experience by asking qualifying questions, such as

- What is your city or ZIP code location?
- Which products do you currently own?
- What time did you arrive? (if to retail, hospitality, or entertainment business)
- What are you doing right now?
- How are you feeling? (just as if they were walking through the front door of the business)

The music streaming service Songza (recently acquired by Google) is a prime example of how a business can empower consumer control over the content they want to see, or in this case, hear. Songza's Concierge service meets users with a timely greeting and three-step navigation that leads them to a song list that is most appropriate for the user-defined moment. As shown in Figure 13.2, Songza presents six activity types that are most likely to define a user's current situation and then narrows the user's playlist options based on genre and a detailed playlist description. If Concierge is not how the user would like to discover a playlist, a more traditional option empowers users to find a playlist by other qualified categories such as moods, genres, and decades. It also allows them to see which playlists their friends are listening to and organize favorite recent playlists.

While enabling a website or mobile application to be used as a search tool can provide utility to customers, there is the additional opportunity for a business to drive sales through being a discoverability tool. The general opportunity with a concierge-like user experience is for a business to reserve so many assumptions about customers, instead surrendering to the customer to define their needs and wants. Think about when you and your spouse, or a friend, have felt hungry but can't decide where or what to eat. Can you help customers find what they want if they describe how they are feeling, how they would like to feel, or provide other prescriptive details about their current disposition and situation? Many food and beverage discovery apps do this, taking into account location, ratings, and qualities such as family friendly or romantic. We would argue that most businesses can take a holistic approach to defining how their products and services align with lifestyles to provide a more meaningful user experience. As the technology behind these apps fades into the background, their everyday utility becomes more and more apparent to the mainstream mobile consumer.

Figure 13.2 *The Songza user interface*

Paul Janowitz, CEO of Sentient Services, works with many Fortune 50 brands in assessing the usability of digital assets such as websites and apps. He told us, "You need to strip out everything that is extraneous, as this is about activity, not impressions. We see how quickly most users want to filter, decide, and choose." The key in doing all of this is to understand that when you go from an online experience to a mobile experience, you are reducing the amount of content, and the app or site must ease the amount *friction* in that *moment*. A big fear that people often have in online shopping and purchasing is *"What didn't I see? What else do I need to look at?"* It is difficult to duplicate that experience on a small screen or a mobile screen. Marketers must take away that fear and reassure both known and prospective customers that they have the right product, service, or solution for what that person is doing at that moment. That is also where reviews and immediate feedback can become a huge influence in a mobile experience. To know that it is not about *missing anything* but rather it simply is about having a narrow field of relevant and/or personalized options to select in the moment is a promise of mobile technology use and systems integration.

The upside of being personalized and relevant to a mobile user has little to do with what happens on the device. Marketers must know where the experience begins. All media, both offline and online, is now employed to drive the experience, due to the pervasive ubiquity of the smartphone. It is everywhere all the time, a reality that must be considered when a marketer plans television and radio advertising, outdoor media placement, direct mail programs, and social media efforts. Transmedia, not simply cross-platform, thinking must be applied to create compelling design, media experience, and calls to action that have users reaching for their device. And then, what is discovered on the smaller, more personal screen must be ready for that visitor in the contextual moment.

Sentient's Janowitz states, "People talk about a mobile first strategy. I think it's the wrong term. It is *user first* strategy, which happens to be defined by when a user is accessing that content, or that experience, or that brand right now. You can see it coming with car manufacturers, that it's going to be accessed in the car, on the phone, on the TV, on a watch, and not all of these are necessarily mobile. There are multiple streams and multiple experiences, and it's got to be responsive and contextual." The key, according to Janowitz, is to look beyond screen size or responsive design, and take time, location, and situation response into consideration as well.

As the use of mobile devices continues to allow people to find, discover, and solve their daily needs and wants, there is no doubt that expectations will also grow for finding specific and exact answers and purchase pathways. Those brands that strive to learn who their ideal customers are, defined by personal preference and the goods and services they purchase and/or intend to purchase, will simply have a greater potential to drive more purchase traffic and sales.

14

Going Local

One of the many key differences between desktop and mobile (digital) marketing is understanding the unlimited value of location. Digital is in parentheses here, as location-based marketing is not only a digital responsibility, as many app developers and agencies would want you to believe. Location-based marketing is nothing new to marketing, and the importance of location in driving sales is as old as time itself. There are many ways that traditional and analog or offline media play into the mobile marketing mix, and when it comes to thinking local as a brand, and leveraging what's possible with mobile and social technology, there are a number of critical concerns to keep in focus.

Ignoring the where and when that often help define a person's disposition to buy can lead a business to miss some of its biggest opportunities to attract new and existing customers to an online or offline point of purchase. Smartphones are fast becoming the primary tool for search and discovery for every segment of retail and service-based business you can imagine.

At the same time, smartphones can be used anywhere to make an online purchase. As has been outlined already, placing certain calls to action and messaging in the line of sight of customers can be an effective way to drive mobile engagement. This includes out-of-home media, outdoor media such as billboards, and transit media that is seen as part of bus shelters and within or on vehicles. In those nondigital forms, each of these media can include specific URLs or phone numbers that correspond with the location of the media placed. This can enable a business to attribute traffic and inquiries to those originating touch points. Direct mail is another powerful way to reconcile an address or ZIP code with an inbound website visit from a mobile device, phone, or computer.

Broadcast media such as radio and television can also be location-based in many different ways. For the better part of the twentieth century, broadcast media could be orchestrated so that specific messages and advertising treatments were seen or heard in only certain markets and at certain times. This same practice can very well be the points at which a mobile inquiry and experience may start, knowing that such moments are happening in a certain location with surety of a location-based media buy. A business can also track and monitor the effectiveness of broadcast media by detecting the origination of a mobile website visit or app usage through an IP address or GPS coordinates, provided by a smartphone or tablet's *location services*. Again, the fact that few people go anywhere without their mobile phone is reason enough to use more media than simply that which is digital and consumed or used on a device.

Social - Local - Mobile

Now that the majority of social media consumption and use happens on smartphones, so much of the location-based content that users are pushing into social networks now influences the offline behavior and purchasing tendencies of those users' friends and followers. Even searching for businesses and ratings or reviews about them has become a popular utility within many social networks. Whether you want to see if your favorite neighborhood burger joint has a deal on its Facebook page or you are researching local car dealerships to see what your friends have to say about them, there is a strong chance that search may begin within Facebook using Facebook Local Search (formerly known as Facebook Nearby), Yelp, and other social networks that provide mobile access through the browser or an application.

For businesses that have multiple locations and/or serve a wide geographic region across multiple cities and metropolitan areas, having multiple brand or profile pages that assume a local or regional stance may be key to driving business. Posting social content that is local may improve the value of social data and conversations that consumers have within social networks such as Facebook and Twitter, especially as smartphones have become the primary device for search and discoverability. In 2009, Expion started with this in mind along with a strong belief that social media could drive traffic and business to specific locations. Expion's senior vice president of client services, Erica McClenny, states, "Companies that have already established local placeholder pages in all social channels possible will have a huge advantage over those that have ignored localized social media. There are so many options for consumers to search based upon GPS coordinates hard-coded to their phones...if you're not available to be found, they will go to a business that is shown to be nearby."

For consumers, these choices might be review-driven and assisted by services such as Yelp, or Google Places, or based upon an open graph search that feeds Facebook results. Also, the more social network users that tag locations in their Facebook updates or interact (comment and like or share updates) with local pages can help increase the likelihood of a business showing up within results in Facebook Local Search. This should continue to shift habits for active mobile users—and ultimately all mobile users—based on integrated data and notifications that each platform and social network puts into its mobile apps. As more and more local searches are shown to be assisted or driven through social media, marketers may find even more compelling reasons to increase their spend on various social channels, as appropriate.

Planning your social content strategy and execution to occur alongside known behaviors and routines is another way that a local audience may be driven to purchase. Expion's McClenny sees that, "Time of day and relevancy of the content matter more now than ever. A broadcast blast in social media does not work as it once did. Asking for a call to action or response is much more critical to keep interaction high and growing an active audience. It cannot be stated enough, the feed of user-generated content to get people to attend an event or stop by for a dinner special is more effective than just high-resolution images that are sent out to the masses. Business must make it feel authentic—consumers of all ages are smarter to the marketing out there. It needs not to feel like a corporate post; it needs to feel like a business has a unique voice by location."

Paying for Action

To fully leverage social media with the mobile user audience, there is also the reality that a brand is almost entirely required to pay for content and advertising to be seen in a mobile newsfeed or content stream. This does not mean that marketers are necessarily required to pay to update or post content to their social network profiles and pages. Yet the decreasing attention span, limited view on smaller screens, and changes to the rules (or algorithms) that dictate what is seen by users have driven up the value of social media impressions. Such advertising and sponsored content also present opportunities to be more relevant and timely, based on location and other qualified behavioral attributes available from users' social graph data. Simply put, the more that people access social media networks through mobile applications, the more those social media networks know about the user, making a media buy more accurate in reaching the user at the right moment and place.

Facebook Ad Exchange helps businesses capitalize on location. Expion's McClenny shares that, "Paid media can be even more effective in supporting underperforming locations or markets with Page Post advertising." She notes the following thought experiment: Consider a restaurant chain with locations in a market where it is too expensive to run radio that pushes for a Monday night special, typically a slow night. In situations like this, rather than run no advertising at all, one could run a consistent page post ad across those local store pages in Facebook for a small spend that creates awareness within the targeted area. For one restaurant client, this translated into a double digit percentage lift in total sales after four weeks of Facebook ads, which cost $25–$50 per week per page post. Overall, advertising in Facebook can serve a purpose and provide the ease of a distributed message to make multilocation advertising via social media simple.

As McClenny said, it may be a big mistake for a business to think that simply buying online media and advertising in social networks will work for them. It's also dangerous for a business to take as gospel collective, aggregate research for an industry about what times users are online. This is not the same as looking at the average number of vehicles that would pass a billboard per day, or the volume of circulation for newspapers and magazines. When employing advertising as part of your social media efforts, it is important to consider the known behaviors of your customers and those users who have subscribed, like, or follow your accounts. It is critical to look into current usage analytics for a business's known audience on each social network, especially metrics attributed to mobile, to determine the best time of day and day of the week, in addition to location of users, to achieve the best return on those expenses.

The Check-In

With location-based social (LBS) networks such as Foursquare, Yelp, and Path, many early adopters of smartphones and mobile applications found that they could find friends and be recognized and rewarded by the businesses they visited most frequently. LBS apps allow users to check in to a business or event based on their phone's GPS location. Along with that check-in, the user is given the option to share content such as photos and video with other social networks like Facebook or Twitter, many times being met with tips from other users of that LBS app, discount deals, and offers from the business. More recently, purchase incentives were put in front of users as credit cards could be connected to LBS apps to have a discount provided back to the user in the form of a small credit issued on the current month's billing period.

Among the greatest of challenges for many LBS apps was, and still is, a lack of participation from the business side. Despite the fact that this is one way to learn about who a business's best and most frequent customers may be, few stores, restaurants, and other companies closely monitor who has checked in to their business using a location-based social network. On the consumer side, there has always been a concern for privacy, as not everyone feels the need or is comfortable with sharing her or his whereabouts. Related to business apathy, users also have asked "what's in it for me?" when finding that there was little recognition or reward for sharing their whereabouts.

Today, location-sharing benefits and features are widely seen as standard across most mobile apps and many mobile websites. If your business has either a mobile app or a website that is responsive/mobile-friendly, you may be in a position to also make each of those digital assets location-aware, whereby the site or app asks permission to know the GPS coordinates of a user's location. Depending on the version of operating system, including system updates and when a mobile device was manufactured, most smartphones are capable of sharing location with these assets as an increasing number of users have the location services turned on most of the time to enjoy the utility of maps, local search, and proximity-based promotional offers.

Being location-aware when someone lands on your website often makes the difference between making a sale and having a visitor promptly leave your website. By knowing exactly where the user is physically located, you can provide localized content that may win more sales than a mobile-friendly site that provides only national offers and blanket brand messaging. While being more relevant and local to a potential customer may drive more physical traffic, a business may also make operations more efficient by presenting products and items that are available in a nearby physical location and referring the user to a mobile commerce digital point of purchase. This tactic is most likely to succeed when factoring location data in real-time. More businesses should be doing it today.

Additionally, businesses are now indexed by location in mobile search engine queries. There are ways that search engine optimization efforts can help a business be found by interested customers who are nearby or who have entered a city or neighborhood name with other keywords.

Commerce Everywhere

Mobile wallet technologies, as discussed in Chapter 7, "Paying with Your Phone," will also play a major role in bringing customers into a store based on their locations. However, brands must now consider the liberated reality of mobile computing from a smartphone as a point of purchase that requires no specific physical location. Mobile applications for marketplaces, catalogs, and other inventory web stores have already become a common utility on smartphones and tablets for shoppers who have a frequent need for certain merchandised products. This is a trend that is sure to expand in the coming years, as more mobile-empowered consumers and businesses find comfort in the ability to purchase from wherever they may be in a way that saves time and resources, sometimes at a discount due to direct-order efficiencies. "For digital marketers, commerce everywhere enables you to take advantage of digital channels such as video and mobile to drive transactions. By offering information such as product reviews in contextually rich experiences, you can take advantage of taking engagement to a new level by closing the sales loop with a real-time click-to-buy opportunity. Commerce everywhere is all about capturing the hot lead in new, digital channels," says Gartner analyst Allen Weiner.[1]

It bears repeating: Mobile technology is moving fast in terms of the innovative possibilities across all industries and the speed of user adoption. Asif Kahn is the founder of the Location Based Marketing Association, and he travels the world discovering new trends and technologies while exploring the way companies leverage the value of location in marketing and operations. Kahn told us, "One of the things that I really strive to get people to think about and understand is to look at location in a way that's beyond proximity-based payments, beyond what I can do in a store. Tapping my phone and checking out at the register, that's just a different way to pay for the stuff in a place we're already familiar with paying for stuff." For Khan, the bigger opportunity is to take the store anywhere and create the ability for people to buy and transact with a business regardless of where the consumer is, whether they are walking by a billboard or other physical location, or even if they have just been exposed to a television or radio ad.

One of the brands that Kahn admires most is eMart in South Korea: "They are recognized for a campaign that eMart produced with a QR code that was generated by sunlight and shadows in the middle of a main public square. You could just walk up to this thing and scan a QR code and then it connected you to their e-commerce environment. You could buy a product and have it delivered to your house. They didn't stop there, almost if they were saying, 'Look, this is really about

---

1. Allen Weiner, "Adopting a Commerce-Everywhere Strategy," Gartner, October 2012. http://my.gartner.com/portal/server.pt?open=512&objID=202&&PageID=5553&mode=2&in_hi_userid=2&cached=true&resId=2193115&ref=AnalystProfile

taking the transaction to anywhere.'" The next campaign that eMart did recently was on the same "anywhere" premise, where instead of a QR code that was affixed to one location, they launched an airship and flew it around the surrounding streets, and through the interior of a large shopping mall, enticing people to scan the airship and shop from smartphones in the moment.

The idea of bringing a brand to wherever customers are and understanding the value of location and proximity to where a physical point of purchase may be empowers a brand to drive traffic and sales by giving the customer a choice. That choice is between buying through the convenience of e-commerce and having the purchase delivered, or understanding where customers are in the moment and presenting them with an offer and directions to the closest store. It comes down to customer preference, but by putting the commerce opportunity in front of them, a business can engage its customers wherever they happen to be.

When thinking of location, new developments in technology also capitalize on other ambient attributes of where someone is at a certain point in time, such as sounds and distance from a physical item or structure. Mobile intersects with all forms of media, as we have stated before in this book. There is a wide range of audio-based tagging and listening technologies that a brand may employ to identify or engage probable customers. There are many services leveraging such technology to enable radio, television, and location to create calls to action and transactions through a mobile device. With machine-to-machine (M2M) technology beginning to see wider use, there are ways a business may push content and promotional deals to smartphone users or display relevant messaging or calls to action around the user at a particular moment with digital out-of-home media. According to Kahn, Toronto-based Weston has just developed a USB-type widget that a business can plug into the back of a television or other digital screen. People—if nearby with an NFC-enabled phone—can walk up to the screen and be met by personalized content, maybe an offer or a coupon, and just by tapping their phone that content moves from the big screen to their mobile device.

Geofencing is another increasingly popular method for content to be sent to mobile users based on their location. A geofence is a virtual wall or boundary set by having mobile apps or other location services share a mobile device's GPS coordinates or IP address information (from Wi-Fi, cell tower, and dynamic email server IP addresses) with a content server in the cloud. Once the device enters or exits the radius or a defined set of boundaries such as a store, parking lot, or neighborhood, a notification is generated and sent to that device with guiding location information, a coupon or other promotional messages. The notification could be a push message from an active mobile app, an email, text message, or phone call to the device that was detected.

A small business could only wish that it was possible to go into Facebook and configure an ad to show people who are actively running or walking nearby that said, *Hey, finishing up your run? Jog on over to the smoothie shop and get a healthy low-calorie smoothie to finish strong.* Marketers have the data to do that now, but there just aren't the technologies or tools available to make it as easy as that yet.

VinTank's Paul Mabray is seeing great success in combining geofencing with social listening for the wine industry to drive more physical store traffic and sales. Mabray states, "Mobile and location services have definitely increased the funnel as it relates to discovering and segmenting customers that have actually visited a location. Before these services, those customers were invisible." For customer acquisition VinTank has used geofencing coupled with its *Interest Graph* listening capabilities to help wineries identify consumers near their location and then use traditional social media to invite them to visit their tasting rooms. VinTank now helps serve the correct customers to the correct wineries by looking for key factors such as: *Have they mentioned the brand on social media? Have they mentioned competitors' brands on social media? Have they spoken about wine, and how often and with what degree of wine knowledge?* Mabray states, "Some wineries are generating upwards of 10% of their tasting room traffic from these geofenced activations. By bringing in an additional 2 to 20 customers a day, a winery in Napa Valley can generate $90,000 to $900,000 annually."

Certain science fiction movies like Steven Spielberg's 2002 film *Minority Report* can be considered more truth than fiction, when considering that nearly all the digital advertising seen in that movie is possible today. For example, in that movie when someone walks by digital signage in a shopping mall, that person is recognized through a retinal scan and the signage then displays a message specifically tailored for them. Beacon technology, or Low-Energy Bluetooth, is being widely tested in 2014 for a similar retail/advertising experience.

It is obvious that there needs to be fair and responsible use of customer information and respect for privacy for so much of what is possible with technology to be successful over the long-term future, which are issues that experts are still grappling with. However, those businesses to first embrace the advantages of smartphone use and location-specific media to adapt marketing approaches and strategy to be locally relevant and respectful of consumer privacy and security issues are likely to beat those competitors that do not. Mobile technology now allows a business to deliver responsive experiences for customers by the time of day, by the day of the week, and by the device being used regardless of whether that person belongs to a loyalty or rewards program. It is time to be fully aware of the context of the moment, largely defined by location. These moments are more than spans of time, now being defined by who you are, where you just came from, what you did the last time you were here—and all those things that help define the context and the disposition of what can happen next.

15

Email and Text Messaging

Smartphone use has created the ultimate direct and one-to-one communications opportunity between people, companies, and their customers. Direct connections have been around for a long time, as businesses could send warranty return post cards to a mailing list and later offer up "call and order today" instructions to a television audience. What is unique about the smartphone is that messaging and content can be sent and received everywhere and anytime, and those communications can occur through a growing number of channels, applications, and uniquely mobile technologies. When the phone rings or vibrates, or a notification light blinks, many smartphone users jump at the opportunity to see what has arrived, like an angler's reaction to a trophy trout swallowing bait that had been soaking at the bottom of a lake for an hour. Remember the distractions we discussed in Chapter 2, "Mobile Is a Behavior, Not a Technology"?

The most popular desktop activity to migrate to the smartphone is *email*, which is only natural given the number of hours we have all spent at a desktop, sitting for hours with little more than an email client open on that screen. Email is also the primary channel through which a person can be reached on multiple devices—and with smartphones, you can run, but you cannot hide from your business email account. The convenient companionship of a smartphone also means that mobile consumption of email is fast approaching the majority of all email consumption.

Justine Jordan is the director of marketing at Litmus, a Boston-based firm that provides agencies, designers, and marketers around the world with web-based email testing and tracking solutions to test, target, and optimize their campaigns. Jordan states, "Marketers want to know whether or not mobile-optimized email designs outperform typical desktop-optimized email messages. I'm not convinced that we're looking at the right metrics to determine the importance or impact of mobile-optimized email design. We're looking for increases in opens, clicks, conversions, whereas the real improvements are likely in the user experience, which is much harder to measure. A frustrated or unhappy user is probably much less likely to buy, or open emails in the future."

As part of monitoring open rates of email messages across desktop, mobile, and webmail clients, Litmus has a firsthand view of the steady shift of mobile being the primary device through which email is opened. As shown in Figure 15.1, Litmus Email Analytics has tracked a 24% increase in mobile email opens from August 2012 to August 2013.

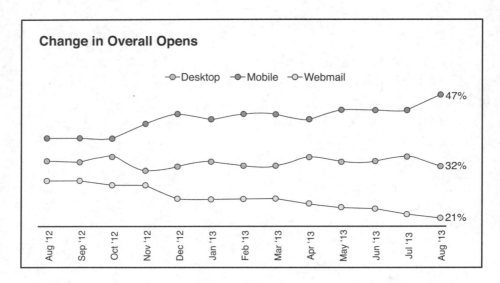

Figure 15.1   *Email open rates across desktop, mobile, and webmail email clients, as calculated from 251 million opens tracked by Litmus Email Analytics in August 2013.*

Jordan adds, "We have data that clearly shows that mobile opens have increased more than 300% since 2011, and that nearly half of all emails are now opened on a mobile device. Marketers must adapt their planning and design process to account for the challenges and opportunities of smaller screens." For marketers, this means testing shorter subject lines and subject lines that are front-loaded with keywords to get their emails opened on smaller screens that can cut off and shorten longer lines. Preview text, the first bit of an email that is visible alongside the subject in a mobile inbox, is also being scrutinized more closely. Mobile users will abandon emails that they can't read and those they find frustrating to interact with. This means that bigger fonts (minimum 16pt) and clear, "tappable" call to action icons (minimum 44px × 44px) are crucial in the body of mobile-delivered email. In addition, choosing a mobile strategy that balances the needs of your team and your audience is a must. A mobile strategy will never be successful if it's not sustainable. This means that businesses should analyze their email opens and other data resources to decide on a mobile approach. Or, as Jordan notes, "Trust the data, not your gut."

To echo what Litmus's Jordan states, while more email is being opened on mobile devices, the rules are changing for when and how email is consumed and acted upon. Marketers must consider the effort that customers and email subscribers go through to read an email. It may be taken into account that many people run to their smartphone when the device vibrates or makes a notification sound. After all, many smartphone users are increasingly dependent and addicted to the distraction as discussed in Chapter 2. To look at this through a behavioral lens, email open rates are most likely affected by the impression that a user has within a few seconds of viewing the inbox. Once that inbox is in view, it should be considered that the smaller screen and a shortened attention span present a challenge to your business getting attention in a busy mobile inbox, where many unread, priority, work, and personal email messages are all competing to be read.

DJ Waldow, coauthor of *Rebel's Guide to Email Marketing,* similarly told us that "the reality is that more and more people are reading email first on a mobile device. This isn't a trend. This will soon be the norm, as the convenience of email anywhere meets the inherent needs of people to stay connected and to communicate." The small screen has greatly impacted design concerns for mobile email. You really have two options, in Waldow's eyes: You can design email campaigns with bigger text so when they are viewed on a mobile device, they are still readable, or, you can design your emails using *responsive design*, a term for a design technique that ensures that the email your company sends will automatically adjust to correctly display, in terms of size and layout, based on the operating system, screen size, and browser being used on the device on which the subscriber is viewing it.

Also, with mobile, *From Name* (that is, who is sending the email) and *Subject Line* become even more critical for viewing and click success. When people look at email on their mobile devices, they are often quickly checking in, or simply scanning subject lines. The quicker that they recognize and trust your name and brand, and the more the subject line grabs their attention, the more likely they are to open the message. While it's not all about email open rates, if a subscriber does not open your email, he is not going to click or take action. "If they don't click, they won't convert," says Waldow.

"Don't Waste My Time"

The increased ability to stay connected and be productive from anywhere at all hours does not mean that your customers, prospects, and newsletter subscribers have more time to sit and read email. The liberation from the desktop that smartphone users enjoy goes hand-in-hand with an increased impatience with poor-performing content, and this is especially true with email and websites. As smartphone users begin to enjoy regaining the time that was formerly lost staring at a desktop monitor, they become more attuned to reducing or avoiding any communications that they deem a waste of time.

A few tips to avoid wasting subscribers' time and, more importantly, how to drive business with email:

- Make subject lines clear calls to action, with an obvious value proposition.
- Use preview text that is legible, as many email management systems default to indecipherable gobbledygook in the header and preview text areas.
- Keep the body of the email short, avoiding large images and multiple paragraphs of text.
- When issuing coupons and discounts, ensure that you are providing a one-click path from the inbox to the browser or to an app.
- Explore ways to have coupons stored in popular mobile wallets, such as Apple Passbook, ISIS Mobile Wallet, and others.

Based on digital media (web, social media, and so on) and general business analytics that are unique to your business, consider the time of day to send an email. If you have the ability to segment subscribers based on their behavior, as discussed in Chapter 9, "Collaboration and Integration Are Critical," and Chapter 10, "Mobile, Media, and Data—Oh My!," consider sending at certain times to certain audiences. For example, let's take a physical retail store with known daily peak times for traffic walking through the door between 4:30 p.m. and 6:30 p.m. and website search activity highest at 3:00 p.m. each day. The best time of day to send email may be between 2:00 p.m. and 4:00 p.m. If, on the other hand, you primarily experience online sales, or e-commerce, you may leverage the same digital metrics as the preceding and notice that your most active windows are in the morning or late evening time periods. This could enable you to send email in "flights" with unique messaging, at certain times, to each audience that shows a propensity to purchase or shop online.

Email can be a powerful recall tool, so always keep in mind the cadence and timing of other communications efforts such as telemarketing, direct mail, broadcast, and social media. Again, make email as actionable as any of your other marketing efforts, as it has a long shelf-life—users can easily search for an email that has been sitting in their inbox or email archives after hearing another marketing message or mention of your brand.

Make it actionable. Avoid sending email to customers or prospects that is purely awareness-driven, or brochure-like. Consider using surveys, polls, and other interactive experiences, as well as sending coupons, recipes, or instructional content that shows customers how to use a product or apply a service.

Mobile Messaging

It is almost impossible for anyone to monitor the speed of innovation and the daily announcements of new mobile technologies being brought to market. There is also a widely held belief by many of today's scientists and technologists that whatever you can dream as possible *is possible,* except maybe for time travel. With an appetite for standing out in a crowded sea of media and messaging, many marketers, executives, and agencies often experiment with mobile technology that they have either read about in a popular publication or seen from competitors. All the while, one of the earliest cellular technologies beyond voice communications is still today among the most powerful: mobile messaging or text messaging.

Developed in the mid-1980s, mobile messaging has grown into one of today's dominant communication tools. Since the early 2000s, short message service (SMS) text messaging has been widely used in marketing, with a recent shift employing multimedia message service (MMS) as it has become popular. MMS extends the 160-character limit of SMS and allows for video, audio, and still image files to be shared between mobile devices.

There are compounding reasons why mobile messaging is one of the most effective ways to reach customers. It is known that almost everyone who owns a mobile phone also carries that device with them at all times. It is also known that 99% of all mobile phones are capable of receiving a mobile message. According to Comscore, 97% of all mobile messages are opened, and 90% of them are opened within 3 minutes of being received. Translated for marketers, mobile messaging is the most direct channel to reach customers, while also being the most immediately received and seen by everyone to whom a message was sent. Indeed, it is the power of mobile messaging around the world that was a factor in Facebook's $19 billion purchase of WhatsApp, an app and service that allows users to send mobile messages anywhere globally without SMS fees.

Mobile messaging is also easier than most mobile tactics to deploy, as it requires a relatively low initial investment and lacks the development and management burdens associated with common technologies such as responsive websites, mobile apps, and most emerging mobile technologies. Despite the efficacy of mobile messaging and its low barriers to use, there are several reasons why it is not a tool that is universally used in marketing. Nick Doulas, chief technology officer at Iris Mobile, told us in an interview that "despite the high effectiveness and easy deployment of messaging campaigns, their use by some marketing agencies and brands is to some degree saturated, and some have their attention turned to other mobile technologies. In particular, the 160-character constraint of basic SMS began to limit many uses of SMS for marketing purposes." The *saturation* to which Doulas refers is akin to email spam, where some brands have become abusive in sending too many messages. It is important to note and respect that mobile messaging is extremely trusted as an intimate communication between mobile users. Between email, social media, and phone calls, few connections between mobile phones can be as direct, immediate, and private as a mobile message.

Iris Mobile was founded by Cezar Kolodziej, Nick Doulas, and Deep Malik, who each spent many years in the telecommunications industry with Motorola, having built out multiple generations of the wireless networks that power today's mobile revolution. Several years ago, they built out some of the more successful SMS and MMS messaging platforms for wireless operators used by consumers around the world. Although SMS and MMS had been successfully used for consumer-to-consumer messaging, they saw big opportunities in applying these technologies to business-to-consumer mobile marketing.

Iris Mobile saw that much of the success of MMS had not been properly extended to business-to-consumer mobile marketing for a couple of reasons. First, unlike SMS, MMS was not being reliably delivered to all wireless networks. Second, standard MMS accounted for the diversity of mobile device screen resolutions and media capabilities by applying generic content adaptation that worked well for ad hoc consumer photographs but produced inconsistent quality results that were not suitable to high-quality branded images and videos with brand logos and coupons. Some business-to-consumer basic MMS solutions were created that essentially relied on a one-size-fits-all approach that too often delivered poor quality content or no content at all.

Doulas goes on to explain, "The possibilities of rich media messaging have allowed the benefits of basic SMS to be amplified by going beyond the basic limits of SMS.

They have allowed similar rich media experiences that are common in other digital media to also be applied to mobile messaging," which has resulted in response rates that are typically two to three times higher than SMS alone.

IKEA strives to continually inspire customers to furnish or update their home décor. In 2012, IKEA launched a cutting-edge mobile initiative that allowed the brand to send home decorating ideas or the latest promotions directly to customer handsets using Iris Mobile's image-based rich media messaging. Through opting customers into the rich media messaging campaign, IKEA showcased a variety of new furniture styles available at its stores by sending the latest sales flyer and promotions directly to customers' mobile devices. This also enabled IKEA to send targeted messages by location across the United States, which helped deliver local, regional offers to customers. IKEA used Iris Mobile's platform to connect with customers in its Family Loyalty Program, where by texting to a short code from their mobile device, customers were able to retrieve their loyalty card information. Figure 15.2 shows the visual experience of this campaign.

Figure 15.2   *Examples of the images shown to IKEA customers through Iris Mobile's rich media messaging platform.*

The IKEA campaign generated phenomenal results. Of all messages delivered, 97% were opened. Results showed that 85% of the customers who participated were using smartphones, which meant that those customers could be driven to the mobile app and website to shop and purchase items seen through the campaign. The campaign was also promoted through online advertising and email, encouraging customers to opt-in by texting to a short code. The campaign also experienced an opt-out rate of less than a 0.5% membership per month, much lower than the industry average.

If your business invested in a mobile app or responsive website, email and mobile messaging can play a critical role in supporting those assets. In the United States, there is the reality that many smartphone owners delete, abandon, or simply do not use most mobile apps within a few weeks after downloading them. Websites are likely to be accessed in times of need or impulse searches. Email and mobile messaging can help sustain interest in both of these assets, as well as driving use and traffic. Location Based Marketing Association's (LMBA) Asif Kahn states that, "The way you fight app apathy is to use SMS and geotargeted SMS in particular. I think you can drive huge activity and traction that's completely location-based; it's completely about driving transactions and offers and deals and all of that over SMS. An app is an app, and it requires marketing and getting people to download it," adds Kahn, while SMS can simply be turned on by carriers, and offers can happen straight away on any phone, not just smartphones.

Before the carriers bring such a service to market, it is important to respect that the tactics of email and mobile messaging are direct and powerful channels to reach and convert customers.

16

The Mobile Web

Perhaps no debate in mobile marketing is greater than the arguments that pit mobile apps and websites against each other. People who work closer to the code, mainly a reference to engineers and software developers, are often fascinated by the many things possible through "deep-rooting" a mobile application into smartphones to leverage address book access, the camera system, and location services. There is nothing wrong with a marketer aspiring to have a cool app, and in many organizations a mobile app can be the best performing digital channel to drive business. The truth is, however, that no business should risk being caught with a website that does not perform well on mobile devices. After all, smartphones are often used as search devices, meaning that Google or Bing are often the pathway that a prospective or known customer attempts to use to locate a business through the browser or an app, leading to the Web.

A primary challenge for website designers today is the broad and confusing array of devices and operating systems that can be used to access the Internet. When deciding what you want your website to look like and which content and information you want to present there, as well as what actions you want your visitors to take, your marketing know-how is challenged in a new way: You must know about all the possible devices, defined by screen size, connection and processor speed, a limited data plan, and other attributes. These ever-morphing combinations of technology and form factors are only growing and are sure to lead to more complexity, if not widespread confusion.

To address these changes in device use and Internet access, most web developers use at least one or a combination of the design approaches shown in Figure 16.1 to ensure a website performs well on tablets and smartphones:

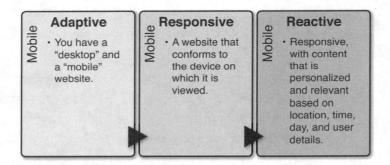

Figure 16.1 *An illustration to show the progressive and developing options for a mobile-optimized website and web content.*

- **Adaptive**—*"With a desktop website that desktop computers and some laptops will see, let's build another, adaptive website that is specifically designed for handheld devices such as smartphones."*

  There are ways to detect inbound traffic to the home URL (web address) for the site, and it is possible to redirect mobile/handheld traffic to the *adaptive* site. This was the first and most popular way to ensure that certain website content could be seen and consumed on a smaller mobile screen. This is also where many companies would anchor the adaptive website to an m.*companyname*.com URL to designate that the site was indeed mobile-friendly.

- **Responsive**—*"Our web analytics show us that we have iPads, Surfaces, large screen Android devices, Windows computers, Google TV, and Microsoft Xbox traffic coming to our site. We need to make sure each visitor is able to use our website on the device he is using to visit us."*

There are improving methods of designing responsive web content experiences with JavaScript, HTML5, and CSS. This enables your website to "form fit" to the device (browser, operating system, and screen size) detected as being used to visit the site. This is also where you can begin to deliver prescribed content to specific devices at certain times on a local basis, at least regional basis. In 2013, Google's algorithm was tweaked to favor those websites that were responsive with one URL, as opposed to having two separate sites with the mobile-optimized designation of m.*companyname*.com.

- **Reactive**—*"We know that we have 100 different customer segments based on socioeconomic, demographic, and cultural data, plus their purchase history, whether they like us on Facebook, and whether they are a member of our loyalty program. To convert more sales, we must leverage all of this to deliver a more personalized experience when they visit our website."*

  This is possible, albeit a little too advanced for most companies as of mid-2014. Through the integration of data and systems that were not built to talk to each other, there is the ability to deliver web content in the moment that leverages responsive design and meets the visitor with an experience that is relevant and tailored with personal details known about the visitor.

For a business to truly deliver personalized, relevant content and utility to mobile users, it will be required to weave existing systems and data together that orchestrate what is seen and acted upon in the moment. For many years now, consumers have accessed digital content in what is referred to as "glance and go" or "in and out" behavior with smartphones. This should be seen as an urgent call for brands to immediately meet the needs of consumers with unique and personal content. The mobile moment, as Tim calls this convergence of data and relevance, must be a well-orchestrated symphony of disparate systems and technologies, as illustrated in Figure 16.2.

Tony Long, technology practice leader for SetUpOperations.com and HealthOperations.com, describes the urgency to meet a user's needs in an interview with the authors: "Nailing the architecture of the website means understanding the flow of data, as a really useful mobile experience has a high degree of data exchange. 'What do we want/need from the user? Do we rely on the user to enter it or can we get it automatically through GPS, contact list, or stored history?'" The perception of speed for a website or an app is driven by how quickly the user perceives feedback, or how quickly the user's input yields a result, making the architecture of the data exchange critical.

The Mobile Moment

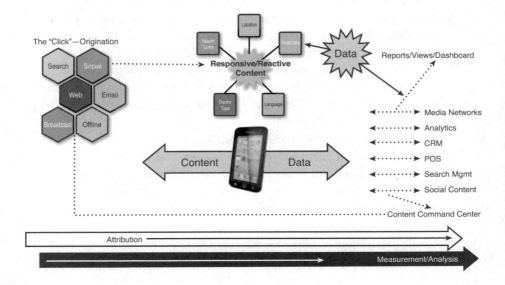

Figure 16.2 *The various systems and data that must work together within seconds of a click to deliver the most relevant and meaningful experience to the mobile user.*

In Figure 16.2 in the top-left corner under *The "Click" Origination*, we listed several digital and offline starting points for the mobile experience or moment. These include and certainly are not limited to search engines, social media, websites, email, broadcast, or other offline media such as outdoor or print advertising. Mastering this user experience requires a balance between the online and offline states of the user, where the physical environment, situation, time of day, and other coordinates may be considered. Long explains, "The user experience starts when the website is navigated to, or when an app is started. This means there is a period of time, most likely seconds of time, perhaps longer, that the user is not yet seeing content for which they searched or expected to see." It is incumbent on the technologist to create a solution for storing and accessing data or some other asset base for the user experience, while the design team needs to craft an experience that leverages these in-between times to create a great user experience. The front-end development team needs to enforce, and deliver, excellence relative to the user's context, based on both known and learned data within that moment. What is delivered to the screen needs to take into account the screen size, resolution, and orientation of the user's device. It must also consider the user's context, whether or not they are moving, and what their data transfer speeds are.

And there is more to consider here as all this leads to the need for a strategist and a technologist to deliver a healthy dose of reality to the design team on what should be onscreen in any given situation. Another key question that marketers are asking themselves is how to replicate what is seen by mobile users in terms of design and content from a desktop or tablet website to a mobile/smartphone website. Here, it is important for the marketer to respect that many known or prospective customers visiting a website have not ever seen the immaculate presentation that a designer planned for larger formats. Thus the user does not care whether the hero image becomes deemphasized or goes away in the mobile version. Today's multiple-device users primarily care only that on a mobile device the content and utility experience load and perform fast and in a way that delivers a rich experience.

Today, all of this may be intimidating to a business with little technology in place and to the enterprise marketer who does not enjoy cross-company collaboration between operations, technology, and marketing departments. The good news is that there are developers and software companies bringing tools to market that enable organizations to more efficiently manage websites and content.

Steffan Berelowitz, CEO and founder of Bluetrain.io, told us in an interview, "We already know that we've seen a massive rise with smartphones. We know that we're in the middle of revolution in tablets. Tablets can be considered the second wave of mobile, which I believe is much more important than anyone realized. Tablets are the fastest growing device in the home and in the workplace, and more people are starting to see the future of the desktop with a laptop as a work-productivity device." This means that there's a real challenge for consumer marketers to create websites that look good, and work well, across a range of different devices—and that is a daunting challenge indeed.

The first wave of web management solutions were mobile-only or adaptive and did not entirely solve the growing problem of being ready for any device a consumer may be using. Bluetrain's Berelowitz continues, "It may have even contributed to the problem. Because those mobile sites are often disconnected from the user experience and the content of a brand's main website, these sites sometimes created more disjointed experiences. For example, you receive an email with a link to a web page that is not mobile-optimized, and then you do not see the content that the person was intending to share with you."

There is now the compounded challenge of tablet use, which many marketers and earlier adopters have targeted to create smoother, more desktop-like, mobile experiences. Now, with some tablets in their third and fourth iterations, there is a dizzying array of screen sizes and shapes to plan for. It is critical for every business to know that, although we are in the middle of a new wave of tablet and smartphone adoption, we are also seeing that the future will have more people accessing web content not only on those devices and desktops, but that there will also be web content consumption via other devices such as flat screen televisions, in-car displays, and wearable technology, such as Google Glass and Samsung Galaxy Gear. To further confuse marketers, Edison Research offers these two incredible statistics:

- More than half of U.S. 12- to 24-year-olds use their video game devices as much to surf the Web as they do to play games.[1]
- More than half of the televisions in the United States are connected to the Internet, often through a connected device such as a digital video recorder, gaming device, or home entertainment system.[2]

Generating Mobile Web Traffic

Once you have invested in a website that can be viewed and performs well on a mobile device, there are inherent ways whereby that site will draw more traffic than your desktop website generates.

Mobile Search

Mobile search is used predominantly on smartphones and is responsible for a large amount of all mobile web traffic. Those brands that are delivering up brief, actionable content in response to these searches stand the greatest opportunity to convert search into business. Those who do not optimize a mobile-friendly web presence and do not have mobile search strategy are missing a significant portion of their existing or inquiring audience. All of this falls into the categories of relevance and personalization, as well. This is for a simple reason discussed earlier in this chapter, regarding responsive websites. The major Internet search engines have started to index mobile-friendly websites higher in search queries that originate from mobile devices, as they do not want to assume the blame for referring those searches to a poor mobile web experience. Adam Moore is CEO and cofounder of SpaceCraft, a web-based software tool for creating responsive websites, and has clients experiencing the search benefits of a responsive website. In an interview, he told us the following: "It's true, Google does weight our sites a little higher, because we are responsive. We've just seen absolutely fantastic results, and I think it's composed of two things. We really focus on the structured data component and organizing,

---

1. eMarketer, http://www.emarketer.com/Article/US-Teens-Use-Game-Consoles-More-Internet-than-Gaming/1010647

2. Edison Research and Triton Digital, "The Infinite Dial 2014," http://www.edisonresearch.com/the-infinite-dial-2014/

allowing people to easily go into SpaceCraft to tag and describe their products and services, the images, and the pages the proper way, the way that Bing, Google, Yahoo!, and everybody basically outlined. We followed those rules and didn't do anything crazy, and then we made really efficient mobile-optimized websites that get a high preference on the ranking. At the end of the day, you want to get discovered, and you want to do it as cheaply as possible. We tell clients, almost all small businesses, to 'go in and add products and services as you see fit, update your content as you see fit, and if you do that properly, your results will be good.' That has happened."

The changing world of paid search engine optimization must be considered as mobile use grows. Shift Communication's Christopher Penn states, "It is interesting, and it is not just personalization. It goes deeper than that. It is something you see Google doing a tremendous amount of right now in establishing implicit context." This context is the result of understanding mobile search behavior from a needs and decision perspective. If a search engine knows that you, the user, are on a mobile device, your location and the time of day, there are ways to frame search results based on those coordinates that are more specific to the user's behavior, as illustrated in Figure 16.3.

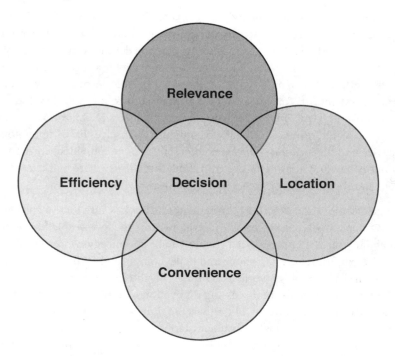

Figure 16.3 *When mobile users employ a search engine from a smartphone, they are most likely attempting to make a decision and act upon that decision.*

The *implicit context* to which Shift's Penn is referring concerns the additional information Google can discern from your mobile device, including location. Penn notes, "If you search Google with the phrase *fast food*, even if you are signed into your Google account on both your mobile device and your desktop, you will get different search results between the two because the mobile device can geo-locate you. It is like Google is implicitly saying, 'If you are looking for fast food on your mobile device, you probably want something to eat,' and it will return different results even on the same personal profile than it would give you at your desk."

From the perspective of Search Engine Optimization (SEO,) SEO itself is going to get harder and harder to optimize for the broad audience because Google is getting better and better at understanding the context in which we use these different devices, and what our mobile behaviors are when we are on those wireless devices. We will see different search results because our behavior is different when we are using those devices, than when we are using our desktop computers or laptops. One can imagine, in the very near future simply walking into a restaurant or retail establishment and having the entire in-store experience reconfigured to suit the context, preferences, and data trail of the individual consumer. In fact, this is all possible now.

What Penn is describing as *implicit context* is readily possible with the Google AdWords platform. You can specify the unique attributes of scripted search results and display advertising if someone is using a mobile device. A marketer may now script a different search result and linked landing page for a specific platform, like iPhone 4, iPhone 5, or LG phones running a specific version of the Android operating system. AdWords also empowers marketers to increase their bid to create clicks from certain ZIP codes. This granularity makes SEO far more difficult to manage, as search results continually reconfigure themselves based upon not only the device and the location of the consumer, but also the individual consumer's previous behavior. Or, as Penn states, "I think that this is where marketers have to understand that the idea of broad SEO is going away."

The rate of innovation described throughout this book is sure to be a challenge for marketers, media, and technology developers for the foreseeable future. But what about your 2015 plans? What should you be specifically concerned about for the near-term future of smartphone and tablet computing? Will Hurley, known by many in the technology world as "whurley," is the chief innovation officer at Chaotic Moon Studios. In discussing innovation with whurley, he told the authors that, "in today's world, not only is the time between technologies getting shorter, but the pace at which consumers adopt them is accelerating as well. This means that timing is more important than ever. Not only do companies need to be increasingly aware of their market timing, but also of everyone else's timing. For example, the release of new phones, operating system updates, and other apps makes for a very large and increasingly complex ecosystem and staying on top of it is a top requirement now more than ever." Consumers now have extremely high expectations of both free and paid applications. They expect apps to be designed and developed in a way that is specific to the device ecosystem (iOS, Android, Win8). Those platforms and frameworks that are not designed bespoke to the device can result in an experience that is suboptimal on all platforms, which will negatively impact both usage and adoption rate.

Beyond search, there is also the opportunity to convert "sideways traffic" from links shared via social media and email, both of which are now primarily accessed via smartphones. One powerful way to do this is to use a URL shortener or "sniffer" technology that converts a click from where the URL was originally shared to an actionable experience on the Web or in a mobile application. This is illustrated in Figure 16.4.

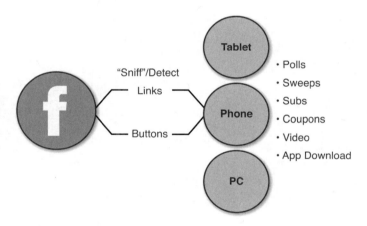

Figure 16.4   *An illustration of how a user may be redirected from social media (Facebook here) to an actionable mobile experience or activity.*

As of the middle of 2014, more than 100 technology companies are testing new ways to connect with smartphones, tablets, and other computing devices. As the speed of innovation and the amount of new devices and software coming to market increases, the most critical direction we can provide to marketers for driving more website traffic is to understand the most current dynamics of search capabilities and digital advertising. In doing so, a competent social media content strategy, a responsive website, and responsive email will be the primary and most successful ways to realize a sustained increase in your web traffic.

17

How to "Think Mobile"

The key to capitalizing on the trends and reality of mobile technology is to think mobile first. Often, businesses consider their existing practices and products and find ways to adapt them to a mobile world. This is just the bare minimum requirement, however, for thinking mobile. The real key to success is not to think about making your existing practices mobile but to understand the ways in which mobility can, will, and should change those practices.

Getting the mobile mindset, then, is all about getting your head out of what you are doing now and into what your customers are doing wherever and whenever they might want or need to interact with you. A great way to do this is to get out of the office! Nothing beats physically retracing the steps of your potential customers in a variety of settings and situations while asking yourself this question: How could we make the customer experience, from initial encounter right through to the final sale, better, easier, faster, or cheaper? Which of our internal processes (and not just how we market) need to change to make that happen? What would surprise and delight a mobile consumer in the moment and create a raving fan for life?

Your company might even engage in some ethnographic research, shadowing people in their homes, workplaces, or other venues to observe and learn from their actual behaviors. Often, the insights that arise from this form of qualitative research are simply unobtainable from desk research. A laundry detergent maker can conduct thousands of wash tests in a lab to tweak and optimize a formula for optimal cleanliness. But it was ethnographic research watching people actually do laundry that led to the spill-proof cap when they saw machine after machine covered in sticky detergent stains.

If you are a retailer, thinking mobile means grappling with a mobile behavior that you might initially resist—showrooming. Yes, consumers are bringing their phones to your stores to compare prices, read reviews, and even "phone a friend" for advice. Ultimately, that behavior could cost you some sales if a better deal is found elsewhere. But consider this: You can't stop the behavior (well, you could build your store in a mobile signal-resistant bunker, but I wouldn't try it). So, given that showrooming is going to occur despite your best efforts, why not *enable* it? How might you take a page from Progressive Insurance and its popular price comparison tool to create the ultimate showrooming experience?

You might find that by removing friction from the showrooming process, and perhaps even facilitating new, in-store behaviors, that some of those sales you were losing to online retailers might fall your way again. The key here is not to fight the behavior of your customers but to adapt to it, and potentially create new, more desirable behaviors. The genie is out of the bottle on showrooming, but we can still enrich the shopping process.

Ultimately, as noted in several places throughout this book, mobile is the glue that connects the online and offline worlds. And perhaps the best way to get into the mobile mindset is to forget about what your product does, or what you want to sell, and instead focus your inquiries on the humans that might interact with you. What are they *doing*? *Where* are they? What do they *want* to do? Simple, yet profound questions. But answering those questions might just lead you not only to enabling a behavior that mobile consumers desire but perhaps even creating a new one that your brand will own, for which your product will always be top-of-mind. The trigger for that action might be a dedicated mobile app; it might be a mobile website; it might even be a simple text. The important thing is the behavior and not the technology.

So, to think mobile you have to be *mobile*. How else can your business learn to think mobile? Here are some guiding principles.

Hire a Mobile Strategist Before a Mobile Technologist

New devices come to market every six months, while platforms and media make changes to functionality on a monthly, sometimes weekly basis. It is all too easy to see such new products and developments as must-have additions to your marketing arsenal. But the mere fact that these devices are somewhat ephemeral and constantly being updated should show the folly of starting with a device or technology strategy. Having an experienced marketer or strategist who knows your business and is charged with following the always-changing nature of mobile technology may give you an advantage over having only a technologist who can author mobile applications and tell you what is and what is not possible. Either hiring or designating a mobile lead on your marketing team may also be a valuable way to monitor these constant developments and help make decisions on when and where to invest in new services and technology.

Aim to Create Behavior, Rather Than Chase It

Technology is extremely pliable, and your business is much more agile than you probably think it is. There are countless ways you can leverage mobility to reach existing and new customers, and deliver experiences unique to your brand. With respect to the opportunities you have to build efficiencies in operations and marketing, look to further those efforts in a way that changes how your customers interact with you and purchase your products or services. This can become a tremendous competitive advantage, as most marketers have historically looked to their peers for validation or imitation. Spend time with creative thinkers and marketers from *outside* your industry to spur ideas for how you can leverage social media and mobile technology to change customer service, create or enable new behaviors, and capitalize on those behaviors.

Stay Fluid

If it has not happened already, your business will be called upon by countless software sales reps and service providers who claim to have the only solution you need or *the* mobile commerce platform that you *must* have. As noted earlier, the pace of technological change is rapid and only going to accelerate. As such, it is a good practice with marketing software, CRM platforms, and other software-as-a-service (SAAS) offerings that relate to your mobile efforts to be careful not to tie your business to a product that might be cutting edge today, but obsolete tomorrow. Be, vigilant with licenses and agreements for these services so that you are not locked into exclusivity clauses, have contract terms longer than one year, and ensure that you are given ownership of all customer data that customers agree to share with your business.

Be Holistic in Strategy and Planning

When integrating mobile technology with business operations and marketing, there are many opportunities to extend current services and to remove steps and friction from existing processes. There will be numerous ways that you can reduce the cost of operations while reaching and serving more customers. The probability of all this being realized is improved through interdepartmental communication and planning. Think of it this way: Both your external audience of customers and critics, *and* your internal team and stakeholders are now armed with a computer that fits within a pocket and accompanies them everywhere. On that device there are multiple channels of communication that can be integrated to better serve all parties in real time. From a marketing standpoint, it is also critical to have all media (digital and nondigital) orchestrated to work together in a collaborative manner.

This means that your mobile messaging can and should be supported with a multitude of other cross-platform messages. It's not enough to simply launch a mobile platform—you want to support that launch with in-store messaging, direct mail, even billboards! *Anything* can have a mobile component.

Never Forget That the Device Is Personal— and Public

For the better part of a century, print media and public relations firms have shown respective advertisers and clients a calculated multiplier for media circulation presented as the *pass-along rate*. For example, a magazine that has 200,000 subscribers may have a pass-along rate of 2.5, making for a total audience of 500,000 impressions that may see your ad or read your story. The magazine could substantiate this number by telling a story about how subscribers either lived in households with an average of two adults and two children, or perhaps subscribers would share their copy of the publication with friends and neighbors. Some publications justified a tenfold increase in impressions per subscription by explaining that some percentage of their subscriber base was offices with waiting rooms.

Mobile, too, has a pass-along rate. Consider PR, for example. Because PR performance is often measured by the volume of sharing a particular piece of content, including stories or press coverage, and word-of-mouth communications like social media are increasingly consumed on mobile devices, then it is time we look at the pass-along rate in a wider scope. While a business can track and measure the distribution of its digital media content, there is the additional mobile opportunity to intentionally drive offline sharing and discussion of social content. Offline word of mouth is still recognized as a powerful way to influence an audience, and you can see examples of how this works any time you are in a restaurant. Next time you are at lunch, take a look around and see how many times someone at a nearby table sees something on his phone and shares it with others. Again, this is yet another example of how something ostensibly digital has offline components that few have even begun to measure.

Think about All the Reasons *Why* Mobile Consumers Aren't at Their Desks

Think about consumers on the go, looking for a place to eat or shop and looking for ways to enhance or enable that experience. But when it learns to think mobile, any business can incorporate mobility into what it provides. After all, mobile can simply be a practical solution rather than just an overall strategic approach. For example, Dell puts QR codes that link to mobile-optimized help guides on the back side of its servers and network products. When the technician is installing it and needs help, he's not at a desk. In fact, he's probably in a server room, but he has his phone handy. Mobile can be a big-thinking strategy. But it can also be a practical, tactical solution to a simple problem. Anticipating and solving those problems where and when your customers have them is another factor in mobile thinking.

Subtract Before You Add

Success stories like the case studies at the end of this chapter aren't necessarily about adding new features or technologies to your existing processes. At the heart of mobility is the fact that mobile customers are *doing something else* when they want to interact with you, and they don't necessarily have access to all the resources and information they might have were they at their desks. With that in mind, the mindset of the mobile marketer should be to remove the need for as much of that information as possible, and to eliminate as many of the hoops that consumers need to jump through as possible, whether that's booking a table at your restaurant or even comparison shopping in your stores. Your first impulse, then, should not be to add functionality to a mobile application, but to subtract anything and everything that hinders mobile users and delays their ability to get or do what they want from you.

We close this chapter by looking at two case studies from companies that really do understand how to think mobile: Intuit and Torchy's Tacos. Both of these companies embraced mobile in more than a channel-specific way; they understood their customers' *mobility* and used it to create more compelling experiences.

Intuit: B2B Mobility

In a B2B capacity, Intuit sees that providing operational efficiencies to its customers is the thing that creates a tighter relationship with them. "Our goal is really to harmonize the user experience, whether you're using a desktop, tablet, mobile device, connected desktop or you're on a plane, it doesn't matter. We want that experience to be seamless," we were told by Adrian Parker, former global head of social, mobile, and emerging media at Intuit. "When we started as an organization, we knew in a B2B sales environment that mobile was an untapped resource. I heard that only a third of B2B marketers have a mobile optimized site or mobile optimized content and less than 25% of them have mobile applications, and we knew as a web-supported software business that we should consider moving in the direction of mobile."

Intuit designed its marketing team with mobile (and social media) baked in from the beginning. Intuit learned that the mobile phone was its customers' preferred point of contact—indeed, before any customer opens an email, gets a call from a sale rep, or sees Intuit's website, most will have a mobile interaction first. So Intuit made sure that everything was mobile-optimized at the start.

Intuit made its decision to move heavily into mobile along several key findings:

- Intuit knew from research that 70% of the accountants who were their clients had a smartphone.

- The majority of these accountants were *connected* and *active* on those devices, not simply just owners of an iPhone or Android device. They were actually using smartphones to share content in social media, or to have conversations with their peers. For Intuit, this presented an opportunity not only to connect with its customers via mobile, but also to empower them to share Intuit content with others.

- The company discovered that 49% percent of the people who were getting trained on QuickBooks, Intuit's accounting software, were doing it at home and not in front of a desktop at work.

- Intuit found that 53% of the people who were taking their training were also utilizing social sharing functions *while* they were doing their training, which further underscored that Intuit's customer base was mobile, away from their desktops, and active in social media.

Intuit incorporated all this learning into a wholly redesigned training and certification experience where customers could actually get QuickBooks-trained and
certified by taking the course on any kind of mobile connected device. As a result,
customers who went through the mobile training certification were more likely to
recommend the product, which Intuit directly attributes to the effects of mobile.
In fact, these certified trainees were twice as likely to recommend the product, and
they were also four and a half times more confident in their use of the product
than those who did not earn a mobile training certification.

For Intuit then thinking mobile wasn't all about the marketing messaging—it was
about taking existing customers and moving them to be advocates and to facilitate
their repeated visits to Intuit for training and additional products.

MAVN and Torchy's Tacos: If You Build It, They Will Spend

When Torchy's Tacos, a Texas-based restaurant, contacted MAVN's Mike Gnagy,
it was to install MAVN's mobile online ordering system, which allowed customers
to place orders using a phone or an iPad for in-store pickup. But Torchy's went
even further: It asked MAVN to connect the ordering system directly to Torchy's
point-of-sale system. Essentially, Torchy's and MAVN wanted to remove as many
barriers as possible between a diner's desire for tacos and getting those tacos.

What MAVN ended up building went against some of the restaurant industry's
received wisdom, because MAVN designers put themselves into the mind of a
mobile consumer to anticipate the settings and situations under which someone
might order online. For instance, while most online ordering systems force the
user to pay online, the Torchy's system allows people the option to either pay
online or simply submit the order without a credit card and then pay when they
get to the restaurant.

MAVN realized that often people would order dinner to pick up while they were
out and about—driving home from work, for example (let's assume while they
were stopped at a light!). A mobile user isn't going to want to pull out a wallet
from his pocket, pull out a credit card, and enter in the number, security code, and
billing information all while waiting for the light to turn. So the Torchy's system
allows mobile users to just thumb over a few basic options, tap Submit, and take
care of the payment once they get to the store.

In the past, restaurants required immediate payment to avoid frivolous or malicious orders, but MAVN's Gnagy estimates the percentage of those to be infini-
tesimally small. After all, said Gnagy in an interview with the authors, "If you get
an order for 500 tacos, you've got the phone number. You can just call them and if

you're like, 'Hey, did you order 500 tacos?' they're going to say, 'I'm sorry, who is this?' and you just don't make [the order]."

Another mobile-driven design decision Torchy's and MAVN made was to engineer a system to save favorites and previous ordering information that was tied to Facebook Connect and not to an onsite login/password system. Again, the thinking was that a mobile diner is not going to want to register or log in when trying to order tacos from the car, but we are always logged in to Facebook. This allows users to quickly access their favorite (sometimes heavily customized) orders without memorizing or entering any additional information. As a side benefit, Torchy's gets demographics from Facebook about its online customers.

What the restaurant discovered was that by removing as much friction as possible from the mobile ordering experience, it quickly became a preferred means of ordering for many people. It certainly removed the obvious obstacles, such as waiting in line, but it also took out some of the other variables in the process, such as repeating a custom order or making sure it was ordered correctly. As maintained earlier in this chapter, Torchy's and MAVN didn't just replicate existing practices on a small screen—they thought mobile first and designed a new experience with mobility, not technology, in mind.

The results speak for themselves: According to Gnagy, the new system rolled out in May 2011 and booked $2,000 worth of online orders in the first month. By 2012, Torchy's was booking nearly *$200,000* a month using the MAVN system.

All Hands on Deck

Finally, we want to reiterate a point made earlier in this chapter: The quickest way to fail at thinking mobile is to confine that thinking to the marketing department or indeed any one function of the enterprise. It may be that the best way to market to the mobile consumer involves an entirely new product or process, or even overhauling the entire customer support function. Everyone who touches your brand internally should have a voice in this process, and the most successful companies will be the ones who can adapt what they do to mobile humans the best—even if it involves substantive changes in the actual product. The companies that will have the most success with developing the mobile mindset will be those organizations that aren't afraid to rethink *everything* about their business—not just marketing, but also product design, operations, and customer service.

In short, the biggest impediment to the mobile mindset isn't budget, talent, or technology. The biggest impediment is fear. Luckily, the best way to overcome mobile reluctance is to have a process and some concrete steps to follow, which is exactly what we will discuss in the next chapter.

18

Ten Steps to Mobilize Your Business

We've talked about mobile strategy and how to think mobile, but what can you do—today? What are the tactical things that you must execute to build a mobility-enabled brand or service?

We put our heads together and came up with ten things you can do today (or, at the latest, tomorrow) to be sure your company is on the right track.

Step 1: Fix Your Website

If your website is not mobile-ready, you are not open for business, period. An alarming number of business websites today still do not even have mobile versions, despite the fact that many of these websites are advertised offline (on billboards, bus stops, and so on). Think about that—if a potential customer sees your web address somewhere around town, what are they going to look it up on?

In practice, there are three options to consider:

- **Mobile adaptive**—This is what companies have been building for the past several years. An adaptive website basically "sniffs" the type of browser or device that the user has and serves the appropriate version of the site. While this ensures that a mobile user gets a mobile-friendly site, it does require your business to maintain two or more separate websites, which for some entities is a recipe for disaster. Still, it's better than no mobile website.

- **Mobile responsive**—A reactive website is where many companies are today. A reactive website uses the latest HTML5 browser language to construct one website that physically conforms to any screen on which the user is viewing the site. This kind of liquid layout looks good on a desktop, a tablet, or an Android or iOS-based mobile phone. While this may require a complete rewrite and redesign of your current website, this is the way to go if you are looking to be mobile-ready *and* eliminate the overhead of having to maintain multiple sites and code repositories.

- **Mobile reactive**—Finally, this is where things are going. If your business is built upon innovation and staying one step ahead of your competitors (and in step with today's early adopters), a mobile reactive website is what you need. A mobile reactive website doesn't simply conform its shape to the user's device but also adapts to the context and location of the user to serve custom, relevant information in the moment to best suit the user's immediate needs. For example, a quick service restaurant might display the nearest location to a user who is consulting the site at home, but if a user is walking by that restaurant at lunchtime, a daily special or offer might be the first thing she sees. A mobile reactive website is truly the best way to take advantage of mobility.

Step 2: Fix Your Content

Mobile-ready content means clear, concise content with obvious calls to action. Again, mobile users are not simply looking for a smaller-screen version of your regular website—they are looking for the things they need from you in the moment, out and about, wherever and whenever they choose to interact with you. This means less text, optimized images, and using video sparingly. Users' needs are different when they are away from their desktops, so consider the time that a mobile user has to conduct an action and the most likely actions the user will want to take, and optimize heavily toward those actions.

Don't forget that mobile humans use their thumbs to interact with your site! Make your calls to action and functionality easy to tap with big, clear icons instead of tiny text links. Always find ways to streamline the amount of information that users need to input to get what they need. Let's never again ask a user to input a ZIP code when we can get their location from their phone!

Step 3: Fix Your Payment System

In the first earnings call of 2014, Starbucks CEO Howard Shultz dropped this tidbit: Ten million customers use the Starbucks mobile app, generating 5 million transactions per week.[1] That's an economy that is likely larger than that of some countries! If your business is transactional, you need to consider just how transformational this could be.

Learn from the examples of Torchy's and MAVN in Chapter 17, "How to 'Think Mobile,'" and find ways to surprise and delight the mobile customer not through what you add to your mobile site but what you take away—like the need to enter credit card information every time or even the need to remove their wallets (and, in some cases, even their phones) from their pockets—to streamline payments. Humans generally take the path of least resistance, and if your business is optimized for the most frictionless mobile payment system you can design, they'll opt for you over your less mobile-savvy competitors nearly every time—if your tacos are good, of course.

Step 4: Don't Forget That Smartphones Are Phones

We use our mobile phones for nearly everything today—navigation, commerce, media consumption, even fitness. Our mobile phones are so powerful, in fact, that it's easy to forget their most basic function—they are phones! If your mobile site requires customers to fill out a web form to get customer service, you are creating hurdles for your customers that don't really make sense in the world of mobility. The best way to eliminate friction in this process? A click-to-call button.

---

1. http://www.forbes.com/sites/stevenbertoni/2014/02/21/how-do-you-win-the-mobile-wallet-war-be-like-starbucks/

Step 5: Consider Judicious Use of SMS

Another basic function that all smartphones have in common besides basic telephony is the capability to send—and receive—SMS text messages. Even if you don't have a custom mobile app, you can replicate all the functionality of one with a well-designed mobile responsive website and a few well-thought-out SMS interactions.

SMS notifications are wonderful ways to send things like confirmations of quick orders or purchases, or any time-sensitive information. Texting me when my pizza is coming out of the oven is a thoughtful way to help me plan my commute home, for instance. Because an SMS is immediate (unlike an email, which even when pushed to your phone you might not read right away), it is also a wonderful way to provide any kind of information that a customer might need immediately. For instance, there are many benefits to the mobile travel itinerary manager TripIt, but we can assure you, none are more welcome than getting a text after the first leg of a tight connection telling you exactly what gate to go to next. For information like this, the best solution isn't necessarily the most high-tech option; it's the most immediate option.

Also, don't forget SMS's richer (media) cousin, the MMS. The capability of MMS to send and receive images and video is a great way to deliver a mobile coupon, or even a quick how-to video for a mobile user trying to tune a carburetor or fix a valve in the toilet.

But in all these cases, it's not about having an SMS or MMS strategy. It's about finding the easiest, most friction-free way to give customers what they want, when and where they want it.

SMS and MMS are also not simply for one-way communication. Text messages are wonderful ways for your customers to provide instant feedback, and this is changing the way that market researchers like Tom are collecting data and gleaning consumer insights. There is no better time to collect customer satisfaction data, for instance, than immediately following a transaction—and that can be as simple as a one-question survey, delivered by SMS, that can be answered via a short text back from the user.

As a bonus, that text comes from a unique human, with a unique phone number that can be matched to a CRM database to provide demographic information and other data that the customer doesn't need to reenter for you and can instead focus on the simple question or questions you would most like contextual information on.

Step 6: Optimize Your Emails for Mobility

After talking and texting, emailing is the third most common use for smartphones, and a mobile-ready business needs to think differently about its mobile emails. First of all, consider your subject lines. The next time you look at your mobile email client, take a look at the subject lines of each email. Can you read them all or are some of them truncated? Chances are most of them are not fully displayed, which can hide vital information (including that important offer you have, which is the reason to open the email in the first place!).

With that in mind, make sure that your subject lines are as short as they can possibly be with the value proposition right up front. And this applies to the rest of the email as well. It should go without saying by now that your mobile-ready emails should be concise and clear, because they are being read at stoplights (sadly). Keep images clean and use them sparingly—you want that email to load quickly!—and avoid multiple long paragraphs of text.

Just as you would with your mobile website, be sure that your calls to action in mobile emails are represented in easy-to-click/thumb buttons or icons and avoid requiring customers or prospects to enter in details. The path from email to app or browser to take advantage of your offer should be one click and no more. Consider how an airline sends an email to you prior to a flight, with very little text and a large button emblazoned with *check in now*. As you touch that button with your thumb, you are then directly sent to a responsive site or app that has your confirmation number or frequent flier number pre-populated in a field. Keep your weekly newsletters or sales promotions to known customers and subscribers simple, brief and, direct.

Another aspect of mobile email to remember, of course, is that the mobile device might be the first time an email is consumed, but it can stick around for a while (how many of you really maintain inbox zero?). So while it is a great way to distribute time-sensitive information, don't forget that mobile content can also be evergreen content, or a resource that is left in a user's email client (or saved to Evernote) for later use. An updated offer, as heard from a radio ad or seen on a mall kiosk, can easily trigger the consumer to go back and search their email archives directly from their mobile devices to retrieve an offer.

Finally, make sure that your preview text (the brief snippet of the body of an email that your email client shows before you open the message) is short, simple, and free of machine language (the gobbledygook from an email's message header that helps an email client parse and display the message). You want your customers to see your offer and the value it provides and little else.

Step 7: Be Sure Your Offline Presence Is Ready for Mobility

Every offline interaction or message your business presents is a mobile opportunity. Remember the billboards that City Year used to promote its Twitter account from Chapter 10, "Mobile, Media, and Data—Oh My!"? Mobility breathes new life into out-of-home messaging, bus sides, kiosks, bumper stickers, and fliers.

Anywhere your message can be seen is an opportunity for mobility, because any offline message can have a URL, SMS shortcode, or QR (Quick Response) code associated with it. Just remember: In every context that you can embed such a message or mobile call to action, consider the specific context of the user.

You now have a wonderful opportunity to know which half of your marketing is working, to paraphrase John Wanamaker, who started the first department store back in 1876,[2] by making each QR code or URL unique to each advertising or marketing vehicle. Mobility provides a way to make all advertising accountable (not just your digital advertising) with personalized URLs and calls to action that tell you exactly which poster or radio spot drove the most action.

Mobility also applies to things like direct mail. Direct mail is already remarkably effective for some businesses, and the inclusion of mobile-ready URLs or QR codes to provide mobile offers is yet another way to both increase the effectiveness of the channel and improve your ability to measure its effectiveness. A direct mail piece might do nothing more than provide a simple way to transfer a coupon to a user's phone (obviating the need to carry around a packet of paper) to be useful and provide value to a customer. And by the way—if you use a QR code, don't forget to provide an alternate mobile URL and/or an instruction. Not everyone knows how to or is equipped to read a QR code!

Similarly, a trade show or other form of experiential marketing gains a whole new life thanks to the power of mobility. Mobile-ready calls to action at a trade show booth or kiosk provide businesses with enhanced lead-capture capabilities and even a way to offer attendees polls and surveys to increase engagement and offer feedback. An experiential marketing event can now be measured more effectively and reliably thanks to smartphone-enabled attendees. You also have the opportunity to build unique, event-specific mobile features and benefits for attendees, such as custom calls to action for information, enhanced ways to follow along and interact with presentations (and other attendees), and even, of course, a way to take selfies with your fellow participants.

---

2. Wikipedia, http://en.wikipedia.org/wiki/John_Wanamaker

Finally, these strategies don't just apply to visual messages but to audio and video as well. Radio is a particularly effective and efficient way to reach consumers in transition and drive them to take action (especially to patronize local businesses). Your radio messaging should include mobile-friendly calls to action to remove as much friction as possible between a listener hearing your message and actually taking action. Radio stations and sales teams, as well, should fully embrace mobility and mobile functionality in all of their campaign ideas for clients—after all, being able to tell that a listener downloaded an app, used a campaign-specific code, or visited a custom mobile URL is the best way to make radio advertising every bit as accountable as Google AdWords.

Step 8: Make Sure Your Video Is Mobile Friendly

Earlier we noted that mobile video should be used sparingly and kept short, but video is an enormously effective way to reach consumers, and doubly so via a mobile device. So how can your company be mobile-ready *and* video-friendly?

The short answer is YouTube, which is not only mobile-ready out of the box but also offers your business multiple ways to interact with and measure your audience, and encourages them to take video-enhanced calls to action. With that in mind, here are some tips to make your YouTube videos ready for mobility today:

- Keep them short! Think about why someone might be watching your video on a mobile device and drive directly to the point, ruthlessly paring away nonessential material.
- If there is text in your video, make sure it is used sparingly and the font size is large enough to be seen when the video is viewed on the smaller screen of a mobile phone.
- Similarly, make in-video URLs as large as possible to be seen and "print" on the retinas of a mobile user.
- If there is a URL in the description of your video, make sure it is at the beginning of that description to improve your click-through rate (and not lost "below the fold" of the More button.)
- Make judicious use of close-ups (and remove images or screens that require users to use a magnifying glass when they are viewing them on a smartphone).
- Clean up your audio quality and reduce background noise as much as possible to account for the varying environmental situations in which a mobile user might watch your video. Video can be a powerful way to share information, content, or even just a funny cat video—and don't forget the pass-along nature of mobile video.

Step 9: Make Sure Your Social Media Is Mobile

If you share content via social media platforms such as Facebook and Twitter, make sure that that content (and any website URLs you share) are mobile ready, or you could lose half your audience! That goes for videos, images, and even infographics.

Mobile and social are inextricably tied together, and any mobile content that you currently have that is not optimized for mobile sharing via social media is a lost opportunity to get more out of your content.

Also, be clear about the action that a social post implies or is meant to compel: Whatever that action is, the flow to that action should be direct and accessible via one click. If the thing you really want them to see is behind an interstitial page, you could lose a significant portion of the users you are seeking to attract. Make sure your social links go directly where you want your users and prospects to go, or directly enable the action you want them to take.

Make sure your social images and visual storytelling are optimized for mobile. Your camera might take rectangular pictures, but the second-leading mobile social network in America is Instagram, and Instagram's photos are square, not rectangular. Be sure your images are optimized for download speed, but of the highest quality you can muster.

Finally, don't forget about location data! Finding incentives to entice mobile social users to append their location data to their social posts is not only like free advertising for your business, but also provides a richer layer of data about mobile consumer behavior for your business to mine.

Step 10: Play Nice with Others

As all of that mobile big data and new ways to reach your customers starts to mature, do not forget that mobility isn't simply a digital or mobile responsibility. Gather the direct mail team and the social media coordinator (or community manager) with your agency's creative director and the PR firm. It is not simply technology integration that makes your mobile marketing and sales efforts a success.

It is paramount that anyone serving in a marketing function starts to understand coordinating events and media to be planned and placed to happen at the same time, in the same places and that everyone charged with managing such efforts is sharing information with each other. Real-time marketing is not limited to a crafty Twitter hashtag used during a televised event, and the only way a marketing agency or department will be able to keep up with the speed of the customer (faster than innovation alone) is to communicate on a consistent, frequent basis.

Consumer attention is dissipating, screens are getting smaller, and information is accessible from the pockets of the majority of the world. With that level of connectivity and communications only broadening, you must solve problems and make decisions more quickly, entertain consumers quickly, regardless of their screens' size, and provide customers with delight in a moment's notice.

19

Science Fiction Is No Longer Fiction

As we made clear throughout this book, what has changed the most over the past few years is not simply mobile technology, but what people can do when they are mobile and experiencing their everyday lives. This space is changing so rapidly, in fact, that a book about mobile technology is obsolete before it even gets published—which is why we steadfastly focused on mobile behavior instead.

What is most remarkable about the continuing refinements to apps and mobile-enabled websites is just how rapidly and seamlessly updates to those apps enable new behaviors in humans. Some of these new behaviors would have been nearly indistinguishable from magic even a few short years ago. Mobile devices now enable humans to integrate aspects of their personal data and information wherever they are and can genuinely be said to be making our lives easier and better—and that's not a sales pitch! Even we, the authors of this book, continue to be surprised almost daily at the new functions, features, or capabilities that even familiar apps offer following an update.

One of the most exciting aspects of mobile technology is the rapidly accelerating ability to integrate information across apps and services, and how that ability is rewiring our brains. Apps like GoToMeeting from Citrix, which allows mobile users to attend and host online meetings using their smartphone or tablet, now integrate with your personal calendar and automatically pull meeting invite information from your email. You'll soon never need to remember meeting numbers, logins, or teleconference information ever again.

To get a glimpse of the future, you only need to look at what some of the current crop of apps allow mobile users to do today and extrapolate from there. For example, there is a whole new group of apps that are essentially rewriting expectations on one of the most basic business and personal needs—the calendar. Smartphones have always had a calendar function that allows users to enter time- or date-sensitive information. But today, apps like Tempo are completely changing the expectations of what we believe we can do with our phones.

Tempo integrates information from your calendar, your location, your email, and even your social networking contacts and friends into one personal assistant app that not only removes the need to hop back and forth between multiple apps, but also smartly assembles all the data you need in the moment of a given appointment or meeting. For example, if you have a conference call scheduled with a prospect at 3:00 p.m., Tempo does not just record the meeting time but also pulls the conference call information from an email for one-touch access, provides recent communications with that prospect from social media and email, and even gives directions and weather as relevant.

What this kind of integration does (as most transformational technology does) is make the technology *disappear*. As apps like Tempo integrate and present contextually relevant information for humans where and when they need it, the technology essentially falls away, allowing people to focus on what they are doing, and not on hunting for things they might need (or trying to remember what they have forgotten). Indeed, Tempo is a great example of an app that starts with what people are doing (or are likely to need) when they look at a calendar in the first place and not merely with flashy technology.

Integrating information intelligently and contextually is one of mobile's most exciting emergent capabilities. Apps like IFTTT (If This, Then That) allow non-programmers to tie disparate services together to handle data in ways formerly impossible for anyone but a developer. IFTTT enables the creation of recipes (not programs) that can make rules-based decisions on how to handle any piece of data, from automatically filing emails from your boss into Evernote, to adding messages from any app with "ToDo" in the subject line automatically to a task application.

And while these capabilities have been available in desktop computing, it is the ability to do these things (and access just the right information at just the right time) wherever and whenever you need to that makes the mobile device increasingly the device that humans rely on for the center of all their communication needs.

In the future, one can imagine our mobile devices predicting our behavior, but today, they can do something almost as powerful (and nearly indistinguishable): Anticipate our needs based on prior actions. For example, an app called Bandsintown integrates listening data from music apps and services like iTunes, Pandora, and Spotify with calendar, location, and venue data to alert you to when your favorite bands (determined by the app, through playlist data) are coming to your local area. This may seem like a simple idea, but that makes it no less meaningful and a powerful harbinger of things to come. If an app can "listen" to what you are listening to and predict that you'll want to see a particular band when it comes to town, it isn't much of a stretch to imagine other things you may likely want to do in the future given your past preferences. Imagine expressing an intention to visit a favorite city, for example, and having reservations for restaurants, event tickets, lodging, and other information "automagically" assembled by a concierge that fits in your pocket. Again, as our mobile devices become increasingly more sophisticated about the types of information they can assemble and integrate, the technology required to do those things falls away, and the users are engaging in behaviors naturally, every day, that they didn't even know were possible (or that they needed) just a couple of short years ago.

Another new app called Wonder neatly sums up just how transformational—and behavior-altering—mobile technology can be. Tim recently discovered this app, which at its core is a gifting service. The premise is simple: Wonder integrates your address book with your Facebook data and effectively learns where your friends live and when their birthdays are. Every day, Wonder lets you know the birthdays for that day and also the ones coming up in the near future. By integrating location data from your friends' profiles with Foursquare location data, the app can find restaurants, retail locations, or other services in the locations where your friends live and allow you to send your friends virtual gift cards for those locations.

What is disruptive about Wonder, however, is that functionally there is no gift card. You register a credit card with Wonder, and you can give a gift card to any venue, anywhere—whether that venue has a gift card program or not. You can send a gift via SMS or email to a friend in Columbus, Ohio, for $25 at Ginny's Wonderful Ice Cream, for example. The moment you do that, all your friend needs to do is register the credit card he uses the most (or the one he would likely use at Ginny's), and the next time your friend uses that card at Ginny's, that amount is credited toward their purchase.

No actual gift card is created in this transaction, and Ginny's needn't know a thing about it, but it's still a Ginny's Gift Card as far as the recipient is concerned. It could very well be seats at the opera or any other venue or service that takes credit cards.

What is clever about Wonder is that it interacts with Facebook and one of the most popular Facebook activities: seeing the birthdays of your friends and wishing them a happy birthday. Now you can send them a specific, meaningful gift (a drink at their favorite bar, say) and have them use that gift without having to put something in their wallet or even remember a thing.

On the surface, this is a gifting app; however, in keeping with the theme of this chapter, we don't have to walk very far into the future to see that apps like Wonder will not only disrupt the gift card business but also the loyalty card business, period. Wonder, and apps like LevelUp, are essentially providing their customers with baked-in loyalty and gift programs that don't require a card, and even (like TabbedOut) a CRM program that allows businesses to directly contact and provide incentives to their customers without a physical card program.

Furthermore, as our mobile phones integrate more of our personal, preference, and purchase data, these integrative apps will potentially be highly disruptive to entire marketing channels, such as Direct Mail. It isn't much of a leap to see that today's mailed package of local coupons could simply be a direct discount, tied to a phone, to a customer of a local service provider for a service the customer already uses or needs—eliminating the waste inherent in Direct Mail.

What also interests us about Wonder, however, isn't just that it is emblematic of a whole class of apps that will disrupt other industries, but also that these apps have the potential to change human behavior by more than simply making existing behaviors easier. Tim has been using Wonder for several months and has noticed that his friend gift-giving behavior has gone from essentially a Starbucks gift card here and there to a $200 a month habit. Thanks to Facebook, we can visit the profile pages of our friends, see the places they actually enjoy, and give them gifts from those venues. You always know what to give the person who has everything, thanks to that person's Facebook wall.

The Touchless Future

The authors grew up with computers and keyboards—maybe, you did, too. But our children are growing up in a world of tablets and touch-based interfaces. Our friend Mitch Joel often recounts a story of his son walking up to their big-screen TV, putting his fingers on it, and attempting to resize the picture (and proclaiming that it was broken when he couldn't).

Mobility is changing this paradigm once again. Today, as we entrust more of our information into various integrated apps, our payment data is uniquely tied to a mobile device that is not only location aware, but also (thanks to NFC technology) able to transmit and receive messages from our immediate surroundings automatically.

Imagine (and really, thanks to some of the startups discussed in this book, you no longer have to) walking down the street, ducking into your favorite bar, and having your favorite drink placed in front of you without your saying a word. You quaff it and walk out the door not only without removing your wallet, but also without even taking your phone out of your pocket. Just as our children are growing up with touch- and voice-based computing interfaces today, soon we will enjoy widespread, always-on access to computational power without even thinking about it, or even being aware that an app is being used.

This is truly transformational from a human behavior perspective: As apps like Tempo and Wonder give us integrated access to exactly the information we need, at exactly the time and place we need it, our need to think about those things goes away. In other words, our need to place these things into our long-term memory disappears, to be replaced by having technology invisibly place them directly into our short-term memory exactly when we need them.

Think that might have the ability to rewire the human mind? We certainly do.

But think back to the title of this chapter: "Science Fiction Is No Longer Fiction." One of our favorite Sci-Fi movies is *Minority Report*, the futuristic Tom Cruise thriller about a division of the police department called Precog, which is assigned to stop crimes *before* they are committed using a trio of precognitive individuals who can see the events of the future before they take place.

In one of the more memorable scenes, Cruise's character runs through a busy retail area, where his retinas and other biological information are scanned by the surrounding stores and advertisements. Throughout the scene, he is referred to by name by a series of video advertisements and offered products guaranteed to fit or otherwise be perfect for him. Today, we might not be ready to have always-on biometric scanning by our local Old Navy store, but we can essentially do the exact same thing with the current state of mobile technology.

Again, the phone is uniquely tied to a single human (while a desktop browser cookie might not be). It provides advertisers and marketers to whom you have given permission the ability to reach you with a singular, just-in-time offer. That offer can be triggered by your location, thanks to your phone's GPS, or by low-energy Bluetooth in your phone that triggers an action when you enter a similarly equipped retail establishment. You can walk into your favorite store and instantly be reminded of that dress you tried on, or a tie that might go with the suit you bought last time, or the name of that Thai dish you loved last time.

And that makes the science fiction frame for this last chapter more than just a cliché—it's a valuable way to consolidate the ideas of this book and to think about what your brand or business could do...today. Because ultimately the way to prepare for the future of mobility is to think about your own consumer experiences when you are out and about in a restaurant, venue, or retail store. What annoys you? What do you wish you could have? The *current* state of mobile technology likely makes any and all of those things possible *right now*.

It starts with the little things. If you have ever been to your local chain book store, consumer electronics store, or even coffee shop, you have likely been asked to join a membership or loyal customer club. Maybe more than once. Maybe every single time, actually. Don't you wish you could set your own personal browser cookie to stop those requests? We certainly do. Those repeated in-store requests to join loyalty programs can get pretty annoying by the third visit or so. But the current state of mobile technology does, in fact, allow you to not only broadcast to the store that you are either already in the club or do not want to join it, but also to recognize, already, that you are in fact a loyal customer and to then simply just reward you without intrusive requests or forms.

Much of the previous chapter was about truly understanding what your consumers are doing in the moment. It is not about imposing your desires on them in that moment, but enabling or empowering them to do the things they already want to do when they are in or around your venue, or shopping for your product, or even just out with friends. And this turns out to be the most valuable thing *you* can do to prepare your business for the science fiction—really, science fact—of today's mobile consumer: Put yourself in their shoes, in everyday situations, and think about what it is you would want (or not want) to make those situations frictionless.

So think about what your phones can already access. Your phone is uniquely tied to you, so a mobile offer is never wasted. Theoretically it goes exactly to the right person. But more than that, your phone (unlike your desktop computer, or your paper planner) not only knows what you are going to do tomorrow, but also where you are going to do it (in a very real, geographic sense) and where you *are* right now. The way to take advantage of the science fact inherent in this science fiction is not to think about what you want or need to sell mobile-enabled humans (at least, not at first). You need to think about what they are doing, where they are doing it, and what they either need to know to do those things, or what they need to have access to in order to do the things they plan to do tomorrow.

When you frame it like that, it's pretty simple to think with mobility in mind. But that doesn't mean mobility will be simple to plan for and execute. Mobility isn't a marketing channel. A mobile strategy might have been something to plan for in the past, but today's consumers don't divide their lives into desktop lives and mobile lives. There is only what people are doing now and the screen they have in front of them to help them do those things. Helping people do the things they want to do when they are mobile is the key to helping mobile humans.

And that's not about technology—which changes every month—but about understanding, empowering, entertaining, and rewarding humans to engage and interact with your brands when and where those interactions are possible.

So, finally, we leave you with another image from modern science fiction. In the groundbreaking Ridley Scott film *Blade Runner*, advertising was alive and well—as one could see from the dirigibles criss-crossing a dystopian city showing video ads to visit the offworld colonies. While that movie took place in the future, in a sense, those ads are already obsolete and made archaic by today's mobile technology.

Today, the messages being displayed on those airborne billboards could be sent directly to *you* when you visited a venue or took an action that correlated with some kind of dissatisfaction, wanderlust, or restlessness. No blimp required. The only thing you need to do as a brand or business is to break free from brand-centric thinking (what you need to do or sell to make your sales quota) and instead to think about what your customer wants or needs when she is out with friends, out shopping, or indeed anywhere that mobile technology touches. How can you make your customers' lives better? How can you reward them for their offline behavior? How can you enrich their experiences? How can you help them do the things they already want to do, better?

That isn't science fiction. That's mobility.

The technology changes continually—as we said, a book about mobile technology would be obsolete before it was published. But *mobility* is universal. And a relentless focus on mobile humans and fulfilling their needs, wants, and desires is the quickest, most expedient path to realizing our science fiction future. Because, ultimately, the science fiction of mobility isn't fantasy.

It's inevitable.

Index